My
ABSURD
Religion

WRP

My
ABSURD
RELIGION

By Which I Make My Living

STEVE GRAY

For information, contact Steve Gray Ministries, P O Box 380108, Kansas City, Missouri 64138
www.stevegrayministries.com

ISBN 978-1-58047-050-6

Cover design by Claire Ryser
Graphic Design by Randy Keeler / www.keelerinteractive.com

This book is dedicated to the faithful members
of World Revival Church of Kansas City.
You were the first ones to say, "Yes, this is right! Tell the world."
And to my wife, Kathy, who has lived this book with me.

ACKNOWLEDGEMENTS

My heartfelt thanks to the following people who have taken a stand for this vision and encouraged me to pull it out from the depths of my being:

Joel Kilpatrick, you have been my encourager as well as my editor. Your writing skills have sharpened mine just as iron sharpens iron.

Carole Hawkins, your commitment to excellence and willingness to work long, hard hours for free amazes me.

Laura Woodworth, your research and outlines helped lay the foundation.

Randy Keeler, as cover design consultant and formatting artist, no one can match your talent.

Becky Hill, you have been the one watching over everything, as a daughter over her father's business. Well done, Becky. Well done.

Claire Ryser, for designing a front cover that makes me look good—thank you.

CONTENTS

Why Should You Read This Book?

Religion in America influences morality, social attitudes, and even laws. All of us need to know what the religion that steers our country is made of and how it got that way. Is it safe to follow? Is it off track? What would the pioneering believers of the first century write if they took a good look at it? I took a good look at it and wrote down what I saw. This is my absurd religion. It is how I make my living.

INTRODUCTION

My religion has lost its soul. This book is about getting it back. While writing it, I argued with myself. How worthwhile is any attempt to find the soul of the church and raise it from the dead? I have decided to try. We all have to try. Religion in America is in crisis. It needs fixing.

Religion is how I make my living. I preach it. I teach it. I write and sing songs about it. I produce a TV show that is turning religion on its sacred head. I am like a junkyard mechanic foraging through old worn out rusted parts, trying to get this religious jalopy running again. I know that many Americans have given up. They have lost hope that my absurd religion can ever change. I am not losing hope.

Twelve years ago, I was the pastor of a small church in the middle of nowhere that didn't even have a telephone. Like John the Baptist, I have come in from the country wilderness with a fresh message. Neither John nor Jesus preached to the pagan Romans and neither do I. Their fiery messages were aimed squarely at the religious folks of their day. I follow the same pattern, calling the religious in America to make some big changes—quickly—before God removes his presence completely.

I remember a preacher friend in town dropping by to pick up a CD of a recent sermon I had preached. As he was walking back to his car, he turned to me and said, "You know, the other preachers in town are afraid of you."

"Why's that?" I asked.

"Because," he said. "they are afraid you might be right."

I am aware of the criticism I may be up against by exposing the truth. But I am not taking wild swings at someone else's religion. I am trying to rescue my own. I believe it is worth saving rather than deserting.

My religion takes pride in its ability to reach the world, but I don't see the world being reached by it. I see the world being infuriated with it. On the other hand, those who have never set foot in a church are applauding the very things you are about to read. That's why I think I may be on to something.

What we don't need is more of the same religion packaged differently. What we do need is a church that God will attend. Historically, when God attends anything, God things and God events happen.

Here is the way I see it: Most people who don't go to church are not anti-God. They are just anti-religion. Even many who go to church faithfully are fed up with what religion has become. That means the religious machine in our nation is in the hands of just a few people, and as best I can tell, they don't want anything to change. That's why religion in America needs this book.

Let me show you, before you read another page, what an expert theologian I have become. A few years ago, a reporter asked me why most Americans don't go to church. Here is my answer: "They don't go to church (drum roll, please) because they don't want to." Deep, huh? They don't like it. They don't love it. They don't want any more of it. They deserve better. I want to help give it to them.

Steve Gray
August, 2008

My ABSURD Religion

By Which I Make My Living

Writing this book may be the most absurd idea I've ever had. How smart is it to take a giant swing at how I make my living? Then again, who better to call for an upgrade than someone who's been in the thick of it for thirty years?

CHAPTER 1

MY ABSURD RELIGION

C hristianity has become absurd. Most people know it, but don't know what to do about it. Its problems are misdiagnosed and shored up with small solutions. It points the finger and blames others for being too conservative, too liberal, or too this or too that.

In my opinion, most of the fingers are pointed the wrong way. Christians believe and do some absurd things and call it religion. It has become a nonsensical dance set to Christian themes that God will have nothing to do with. The many books written on the subject trot out the same old arguments. Some say the church has become too institutionalized while others say it has become too modern. To me, both sides are missing the point. It's absurd either way. My purpose for writing this book is to share how absurd religion has become, how it got that way and what can be done about it.

Let me give you an example of how religion thinks and how it tries to fix things. Recently a Christian magazine offered a sup- posedly "radical" solution to shrinking church attendance. Its absurd solution was to have all churches start meeting in homes. This writer argued that early Christian churches met in homes and we should too. Of course, some people are so desperate for something real to happen they will try anything. Now we have a bunch of Christians meeting in living rooms across America, kneeling down where the dog peed yesterday, and feeling more spiritual than the rest of us.

" I am not the first to think that religion in America is broken and needs fixing. "

Herein lies the problem. Christians for the most part believe that they have been on the right track for the last five hundred years since the Protestant Reformation. They think all their religion needs is a few tweaks and upgrades to make it work better. I disagree. The absurdities began five hundred years ago and have left the people who want to believe and experience God with empty religion.

I am not the first to think that religion in America is broken and needs fixing. However, many of the books I've read sound anti-God or anti-church, written by someone with a chip on their shoulder or an ax to grind. I assure you that I have neither chip nor ax. Religion is how I make my living. However, after thirty years of trying to make it work, I am tired of following the absurd script that now passes for biblical Christianity.

Let me say up-front that I believe in the God of the Bible. I just don't see him attending most churches. Yet even without any sign of him being there, my religion just keeps marching on.

I knew this religion had some absurdities long before I became a Christian. When I went away to college, I lived "on the wild side" without thinking much about it. Why would complete strangers come to my door and try to convert me? The conversations I had with them were absurd to me and usually went something like this:

(Knock on door)

ME: Yeah?

STRANGER: Are you saved?

ME: Huh?

STRANGER: If you don't know, then you probably aren't.

ME: Know what?

STRANGER: If you were to die today do you know you would go to heaven?

ME: Go to heaven?

STRANGER: Yeah, if you died today would you go to heaven?

ME: I don't know.

STRANGER: Would you like to know how to get into heaven?

ME: If I died?

STRANGER: Yeah, if you died today.

ME: Can I ask you a question?

STRANGER: Sure.

ME: Do you have anything for me if I don't die?

STRANGER: What do you mean?

ME: I don't think I am going to die today. So what have
you got for me if I live? What will God do for me, right
here, right now?
STRANGER: I don't know.
ME: Come back when you find out.

The conversation made no sense to me. I was 21, having
fun, and being crazy—looking for everything and willing to try
anything. "I want to live man. Can you dig it?" was my motto.
The one thing I wanted back then, religion didn't seem to offer
me.

So, when did this absurd religion become my religion?
Strangely enough, it was through my own mother that I got involved. She asked me if I would like to become like the people
I had heard about in the Bible. It had never crossed my mind
that it was even possible, but it did intrigue me. She didn't
mean that all of a sudden I would become some kind of a saintly
person. She meant that I could experience God just as they did
in the Bible. That's all it took. I prayed right there on the spot.
Something did happen. After the prayer I said, "I've been called
to preach," and I've been doing it ever since. I was twenty-three
then and knew nothing about the Bible. One thing I did know:
I knew I didn't want to stand at someone's door with absurd
religion that had nothing to offer the living.

What I have in mind is a lot more revolutionary. I'm daring
people to go back to the roots of the Protestant Reformation
and start all over again. My goal is to show the average Joe and
Jane of America that our five-hundred-year-old religion is full of

absurdities, which can't be fixed by handyman-style repairs. We need an overhaul. We need another reformation.

You see, few Americans are anti-God. They are anti-religion. God is not dividing America. The Bible is not dividing America. Jesus isn't dividing America. Religion with all of its absurdities is dividing America. Since when is it okay to let that continue?

" Religion with all its absurdities is dividing America. Since when is it okay to let that continue? "

Why start over? The Christians of the first century were not Jews, Catholics or Protestants. Nobody knew exactly what they were. All anybody knew was that their religion was new, and it worked. It transformed lives. People experienced the presence of God. They saw the power of God. They were healed. They witnessed miracles. They were never the same afterward. God came down and helped his people. Does that describe our churches today? Hardly. Today lame religion peddles its snake oil to anyone who believes it has the power to "cure what ails ya." Is it any wonder that the real God of heaven is nowhere to be found?

A Young Optimist

I was naïve when I first got started in ministry. Traveling with my singing family on a Greyhound bus hither and yon doing "the Lord's work" seemed like the ideal adventure. I thought it was going to be all about helping ordinary people experience the presence and power of God. It wasn't long though before

I got my wake up call. I remember the first time I was invited to preach at a real church with a real pulpit. Walking in, I felt like Clint Eastwood with a .44 magnum special, ready to free the world from the powers of darkness. I almost felt like saying, "Are you feeling lucky, punk?"

> **" I spent those years engulfed in a mob-ruled, money-hungry, powerless, guilt-mongering, anxiety driven religion that didn't offer people any real help. "**

That night I preached the best I knew how, with great passion and energy. At the conclusion I asked if anyone needed prayer. There I was, a tough young hombre standing tall, ready to fight God's battles. It was my High Noon moment, or so I thought. After preaching my sermon, a few people came down to the front and I began to pray for them. Then an old man walked down the aisle. He leaned forward and whispered in my ear, "I'm dying. I need a miracle. Will you pray for me?" I wanted to. I was ready to. But the moment was interrupted by absurd religion.

An usher handed me a note. It read, "You need to come to the church office now." Puzzled, I left the platform and headed towards the tiny office. The chorus of people singing "Only believe, all things are possible, only believe" faded as I entered. Inside the office were walls covered with ancient-looking books that appeared to have never been read. Standing in a semi-circle were six men. Their faces were drawn in deep concern. I stood waiting, wondering. Finally, a voice broke the silence. "You can't pray for miracles in the church. If you want to pray, you will have to do it outside or on your bus."

These were people who said they believed in God. When did it become against the rules to pray for a miracle in church? How did my religion ever get so absurd?

That incident kindled inside of me a sense of dread for the church scene, even though I kept on ministering with my family for almost seven years. Every church we went to reminded me of what Forrest Gump said, "My momma always said, life was like a box of chocolates. You never know what you're gonna get." With every new church I dreaded facing the absurdities, the stupidities, the prejudices we inevitably found there. Worst of all, even though these were churches, few people had any faith for anything. They didn't want the presence of God or miracles. They wanted control.

I spent those years engulfed in a mob-ruled, money-hungry, powerless, guilt-mongering, anxiety driven religion that didn't offer people any real help. The only thing it had to offer, when all else had failed, was the promise of another life after you died. When a religion relies too much on the promise of another life, it means it has nothing to offer in the here and now life. It's an automatic admission of ineffectiveness.

I got beat up one time in the first grade. It was pretty humiliating. One snowy day, I refused to give up my sled to three much older boys. When the hitting started, my friend ran into his house and locked the door. I followed, but he was too scared to open the door for me. The bigger boys dragged me off the porch and beat me some more. Beatings are no fun. I feel I might be risking another one by writing down my thoughts in this book. The protectors of religion are always ready to pounce on the reformers and refiners of ineffective Christianity. They did it to Jesus when he offered spiritual health to ordinary men and women. They went beyond a beating and actually killed him. He was put to death, but not because of what he said. Rather, it was because of whom he said it to. I may run into the same problem.

You see, if Jesus had called the Romans to change and re-pent, he would have been a national hero. But he called the Jews, God's own followers, to repent. He told the seemingly good guys to change their ways, and they didn't like that. Blinded by their own goodness, they saw no reason to change. Unfortunately, "good" is not the same as "God." Religion can be good and still not have God. Religion is everywhere, but God's real presence is a rare find. When that happens, as I believe it has today, God calls the religious good guys to make changes.

What We Have Lost

Christianity became absurd when it lost the power, provision and presence of God. It has become, for the most part, a man-made club, a theological debating society. In the first century, spiritual men and women could pray and change the world. In America today, religion is spiritually crippled and must resort to politics and legislation to get anything done. Forget prayer. God stopped listening a long time ago.

Even worse, Christians don't recognize or see what has happened. All religions, regardless of name, become absurd when they lose the ability to diagnose their own problems. The prophets of old were like doctors with a stethoscope. They listened, heard from God and declared a remedy. But my religion is so busy maintaining its image that it denies it even has problems.

" Christians deceive themselves into believing that if everyone living outside of Christianity would live moral lives, America would be safe and secure. "

Often, it blames society's woes on people who are not Christians. It rails against the immoral people of America as though they hold all the power of the future. Christians deceive themselves into believing that if everyone living outside of Christianity would live moral lives, America would be safe and secure.

The prophet Jeremiah of the Bible said there are only two sins that cause societal misery. Sin number one is "My people have forsaken me." In other words, God's followers gave up on following. To them, God was no longer a part of the solution, and they simply lost interest in Him. They still did religious things, but only halfheartedly. Remember, God's people committed this sin. It was active religion without a conscience. God wasn't angry that the pagans were acting like pagans. How else would you expect them to act? It would have changed nothing for the pagans to walk a straight line. God's heart was breaking because his own people paid him no mind, though they pretended to. God's response was to withdraw and be hard to find.

This is what I see in the churches of America. People may go to church, but their first question is, "When does this thing get over?" Churches have become like fast food restaurants offering speedy service. Christians don't want the power and presence of God in their lives; they just want to be left alone to get on with their lives. Ask any pastor or minister what the greatest problem of the church is today. It all boils down to one thing: The people just don't care. They want a little bit of God in their lives, but they mainly want food, fun and entertainment. In most cases, religion is giving them what they want.

The second sin from Jeremiah follows on the heels of the first. God says, "You have dug your own cisterns." A cistern in those days would catch rainwater. A cistern was critical to survival. By digging their own cisterns, God's people had stopped looking to him for provision or protection. They felt they could handle it all just fine without his involvement. They could catch the rain all by themselves.

" I believe every human has the right to experience the real presence of God. "

Today, our society with its mind-boggling advances in medicine, the military and social programs keeps most everybody afloat. But these advances do nothing to solve the real crises we face as individuals and as a nation. While promising a glorious afterlife, America's spiritual diet has been reduced to bread and water. No wonder we have so much crime and violence. It always runs rampant and unabated in a spiritually starved society. There is little hope for help from heaven when religious leaders become anorexic in their souls, uninterested in the bread from heaven.

I believe humans want to know God. They want to feel him, hear him, and be able to ask him for help. But most people, even Christians, have given up on the possibility. I hope to change that. I know some of my religious "friends" won't like some of the things I am going to say on the following pages. But I am not doing this for them. I am doing this for you. I believe every human has the right to experience the real presence of God. Every person deserves to have a "God is with me," experience. My religion used to be able to offer that, before it got absurd. My goal for you, the reader, is to reveal some of the things that make God so hard to find for most people, and then to show you how to find him.

My heart says there is more "out there" than we are getting. I am trying to do my part to transform absurd religion into authentic religion. I want to see the power, provision, and presence of God become a part of our everyday lives.

I hope you will join me. I believe it is a journey worth taking and a battle worth fighting.

I am wondering how many will put down this book when they read my interpretation of Martin Luther? I am not sure he is the saint some have thought him to be. Will those steeped in this religion be able to comprehend what this chapter is about? They may see this as a personal attack on Luther, rather than an exposé of the system that he created.

CHAPTER 2

ABSURD REFORMATION

I am a Protestant, which only means I am not a Catholic. Protestants, in my experience, live up to their name: They love to protest. In the Protestant church, if someone doesn't like something, he feels duty bound to rise up in protest. It must be in our blood. If you have attended a Protestant church for any length of time, you already know this.

Martin Luther, known as the father of the Protestant Reformation, created a religion rooted in protest. He planted the idea that if you don't like something, you should leave, take some people with you and start something of your own. At least that's what he did when he got into a disagreement with the Catholics. Consequently, Protestants are not very loyal to each other, and their churches are always splitting over minor doctrinal differences and other "critical" decisions—like which color of carpet to put in the fellowship hall.

I've often wondered why Protestants remain so stubbornly committed to protesting every little thing they dislike. Catholics seldom do this. In the town of twenty thousand people where

I grew up, we had only two Catholic churches. One was for the east side and the other for the west side. These Catholics planned to attend the same church their entire lives.

I realize the Catholic Church at large has had its share of problems, but habitual protesting and splitting is not one of them. I have never known Catholics to hold secret meetings or telephone campaigns to protest the priest. I have never heard of a Catholic Church split. I have never heard of a nun being run out of town by a group of parishioners who didn't get their way.

Yet these things happened all the time among the Protestants. Compared to the two Catholic churches in my town, there were anywhere from eighty to a hundred Protestant churches, depending on how well everyone was getting along. I never went to Wal-Mart without seeing someone I used to go to church with. The hundreds of Protestants in town changed churches or started new ones every few years. They usually left mad and—you guessed it—in protest.

I did not know of one single pastor in that town who had not experienced terrible heartache because of this. You might say that when Martin Luther nailed his protest to the church door in 1517, he split the Catholic Church, and the Protestants have been doing the splits ever since.

Because of this tendency, the religion that should have saved me almost destroyed me. Eleven years ago, I was leading a church in Middle America so small it didn't even have a telephone. Our church building was a typical clapboard structure built in

1859. It looked like the old country church you see on Christmas cards. The situation sounds idyllic, but it was far from that.

Before living in a small town, I had some preconceived ideas about them. I thought small towns were safe and friendly. Like many folks, I let down my guard when I took a drive in the country. I expected Sheriff Andy of Mayberry to be there to keep the peace. By moving to a small town, I hoped to find the simple life of church picnics, potato salad and friendly neighbors.

I never got those things—not even the potato salad. Instead, religious people in town, who called themselves Christians, had rotten things in store for me. These people were raised as run-of-the-mill Protestants and they followed the pattern exactly. What I saw was vicious religion that nailed anyone that got in its way. Add to that the day-to-day dealings with cranky Christians threatening to leave the church if they didn't get their way. They said they believed in grace and forgiveness, but I never actually saw them put those things into practice. As a first-time pastor, nothing had prepared me to go head-to-head with this mean religious bunch. That isn't to say that I didn't have some wonderful friends who stuck it out with me. I wouldn't want them to read this and think I had forgotten. But our good times were often spoiled by the ongoing small town rumor mill.

Anxiety Driven Religion

I'm not a big fan of Luther's theology. I used to be, but not any more after dealing with his protest-happy inheritors. However, Luther did help straighten out one major part of the Catholic Church's theology. From him, we learned the proper way to be forgiven. It didn't involve selling indulgences as the Catholics had been doing. The Catholics had developed the big business of buying your way out of punishment after sinning. Martin Luther gave the world a renewed interest in faith and grace. What he started out with was good, but he didn't take it far enough.'

At the heart and soul of Martin Luther's protest was an obsession with sin. The next time you hear a hellfire preacher railing about sin and damnation, you can thank Luther for it. Luther was driven by anxiety about his own sin and everybody else's, and that led him to search for a formula for sinners to know God's love. His obsession with sin remains the focus of the Protestant movement today.

" The next time you hear a hellfire preacher railing about sin and damnation, you can thank Luther for it. "

For example, if you convert to the Christian faith in a Protestant church, you almost certainly will be required to acknowledge your personal sinfulness—again Luther's formula. The confession of personal sinfulness is followed by the offer of God's grace, which is treated like a sort of spiritual life preserver. That's why the traditional Protestant sermon includes a "Do you know you are a sinner?" section followed by the offer of grace and love. It is a pass-fail system. If the hearer feels no guilt and anxiety, Protestants are at a loss about what to do. They have no Plan B.

I saw a group of young evangelicals doing traditional "street witnessing" one time. Street witnessing is when a Christian tries to create anxiety about sin and the fear of going to hell in somebody. If the person admits he or she is sinful and shows signs of anxiety, the evangelizer talks about God's offer of grace. This group of evangelists looked anything but joyful doing the "Lord's work" that day. They were standing outside a restaurant during happy hour. None of the patrons wanted to stop and listen, and they certainly didn't want to feel guilt-ridden or anxious about their souls. So these eager young Christians were left looking unsure, like gamblers who had just lost a sure bet and were wondering what had happened.

A couple of the guys recognized me, so I asked them what was wrong. They said, "No one wants to hear about Jesus." I replied, "That is where you are wrong. What you mean is no one wants to feel like Martin Luther." The people going into the bar were not anti-God. They were merely anti-sixteenth century religion. They didn't want to feel like Martin Luther had felt as a pre-condition to meet God.

I have found no historical evidence that the preachers of the first century ever used Luther's approach of using guilt to save people. Paul, who wrote two thirds of the New Testament, had another way. He never acknowledged his own sinfulness while evangelizing. He hadn't been converted by being brought to a point of guilt and anxiety, fearing he might go to "the bad place down there." Instead, he was converted when he encountered the presence and power of God Almighty. This power knocked him to the ground. It changed his mind and heart about Jesus. It became his formula for successfully evangelizing others, far removed from the anxiety driven, guilt-ridden formula of Martin Luther.

When Paul spoke, people were brought into the very presence of God. The power of a guilty conscience didn't change him or them. The power of God did—whether or not they felt any guilt about anything. Paul's own words confirm this. "My message and my preaching were not with wise and persuasive words, but with a demonstration of the Spirit's power, so that your faith might not rest on men's wisdom, but on God's power."

What about Jesus? Did he present the gospel to create anxiety and guilt? Was his goal to convince people of personal sin? Most preachers think so. Listen to his message. "Repent (turn toward), for the Kingdom of God is here." He did not stress present sin. He stressed the present kingdom and the need to turn toward it immediately. The question is not whether you recognize your bad past, but rather, are you ready to respond to your good future in the Kingdom of God?

The Jews of Jesus day were a mix of religious levels. Some, like the tax collector in the temple, with great guilt and anxiety beat his chest and cried out for mercy. Others, like most of the religious leaders, had no guilt about anything. The point is this: guilt or no guilt makes no difference to God. He is not looking to see how you feel about your past life. He is looking to see if you will respond today.

Martin Luther lived with a taskmaster who shouted, "You'll never be good enough for God." He desperately needed a formula that, in spite of the voices, made him acceptable. The problem is that feeling accepted is still not the answer. There are plenty of guilty people today, obsessed with their sin and wanting to be accepted who will not respond to God's kingdom offer.

How should someone respond? Jesus said to repent, but does that mean the Martin Luther way—through anxiety, guilt, and acknowledgement of sin? No. Jesus said to repent, which means to turn around or turn another way. He was calling people to turn from every other kingdom, system, or philosophy and towards the present Kingdom of God that was right in front of them. The gospel doesn't start with your remorse or failures. It starts with Jesus and his kingdom coming to you in whatever state you are in. Repentance is more than turning from what was. It is turning to what is. It is turning to a different king, with different ways of thinking and acting. But my religion tells people, "It doesn't matter who you are or what you have done—you can come to Jesus." Then it contradicts itself almost immediately and makes a person confess every bad thing ever said or done. How absurd is that?

Revolution

We need a new starting point. The Protestant Reformation is past its expiration date. Martin Luther's legitimate concerns about how Christianity was carried out were addressed and rectified a long time ago. We no longer need to take theology lessons from a man who picked a fight with the Catholics five hundred years ago. We need a new reformation. We need a new revolution. And the only people who can do it are those who are tired of absurdities, but not tired of God. First, we must have a revolution of faith. This revolution must go beyond personal anxiety and insecurity. It must renew faith in God's power and principles to transform a life. We need to stop acting as if the world is overcome with guilt and anxiety, just wanting some affection from God. The other day I drove by a church sign that read, "God loves you." My reaction was, "Who cares?" Literally—who cares? I don't see the people of America asking if God loves them. I see the people of America wishing for some divine help and unable to get it. Absurd religion still believes that all people are living with Luther's guilt and anxiety and searching to know if God loves them. It continues to offer answers to questions that no one is asking.

" Absurd religion still believes that all people are living with Luther's guilt and anxiety and searching to know if God loves them. "

The real problem now is that the American people have given up on divine help. They are emotionally and spiritually exhausted by religion that does not offer the power of God, but only the message of how much God loves them. This absurdity has run its course and it's time to move beyond it.

Second, we must redefine what a church is. A church is not a place with a steeple, or baptistery or altar. It's not even a place with a pastor or a priest. Neither is it a place to find sympathy or support. A church is a place where people go to experience God. It is to be like no other place on earth. It is the God meeting place. If there is no power or presence of God, then it is not a church. It is something else.

We need a national boycott of powerless religion. I am not content to let the church go for another 500 years with the same baggage Luther saddled us with. An encounter with guilt is no guarantee of an encounter with God. It's time for all of us to sign on to a new revolution, to toss the anxiety-obsessed and guilt-fixated reformation overboard and start over with a first century experience of faith, power and presence. Guilt-full yet power-less religion is absurd.

Can a new reformation, a revolution, take place in religion today? I not only believe so, but I believe millions of people are hoping it will. People are tired of religion that drowns in pessimism. They don't want to be a part of a religion that believes the present evil is too big for us. Nobody wants to follow the battle cry that says, "Join us! We're losers!"

There is, however, a great revival of optimism beginning. I am beginning to feel the rumble of a new reformation released from pessimism. Evil isn't too big for us; it can be defeated. This new reformation is religion without retreat, led by King Jesus who knows no defeat.

According to the Bible, Jesus is no longer the suffering servant on the cross or the humble servant from Galilee. The book of Revelation says Jesus is a warrior with eyes like flames of fire. That is who Jesus is now. He is a king with a kingdom that is active among us right now. This king not only wins battles, he wins every battle until there is no one left standing to fight. This is the victorious Jesus raised from the dead. He is not the Jesus of the Protestant Reformation who is mortified and troubled by our sin and embarrassed by his creation. He is no sissy savior. The Bible says he slays his enemies just by the words that come out of his mouth.

" People are tired of religion that drowns in pessimism. They don't want to be a part of a religion that believes the present evil is too big for us. "

Jesus isn't asking us to feel guilty about ourselves. He is asking us to bow to him. He wants us to feel and to know first-hand his strength and power. Then he wants us to get up and serve him.

Julie's Story

My dad was the pastor of a mainline denominational church. I loved and respected him, but I felt like I was drowning in a multitude of man-made rules and regulations. This strangling legalism caused a mass of confusion within me. Everyone I knew went to a huge church across town. And there I was trapped in my dad's church, completely depressed and feeling like I was in a teensy weensy box with a sealed lid and a big fat bow. I was raised bound by rules that said I had to wear a skirt at all times, couldn't cut my hair, and so on. It was nothing but a set of frustrating laws and regulations. Adhering to those ridiculous mandates didn't make me any more or less spiritual! But no one was even listening to me, much less agreeing.

I remember screaming at God, "I know there's more to you than just a bunch of rules and regulations!" In my heart I knew these couldn't possibly be his requirements.

Things were used to motivate me to be good. "If you're a good girl, God will give you things," my dad would say. So, I would pray in the shower and on my way to work, and honestly do my best to be good. But I got tired of trying to be good all the time. It was exhausting, and virtually impossible for anyone to live up to all those expectations. "It's completely unreasonable to ask that of anyone," I screamed silently. "And it doesn't help anyway!"

In due course I found myself gracing a psychiatrist's sofa, emotionally and psychologically disfigured by religious legalism.

The mother of one of my girlfriends told me, "God is not putting those demands on you– religion is." I later learned her words were true. God is not a hard taskmaster–religion is.

In my desperation to get free from this religious taskmaster, I found a church where they taught the truth of the Bible in a way that set people free from "religion" so they could really experience God's life and presence.

The first service there, the praise and worship leader said, "The presence of God is about to fall in this place!" For the first time in my life, I experienced the living God. What I felt was almost indescribable. His presence was so good and powerful. I felt a sudden freedom, as if the lid had just been taken off my life.

My editor says I am trying to cover too much in this chapter. I think he is right, but then again, there are so many weird religious ideas floating around. I have to remember this is just a start-up book, and not meant to be a commentary.

CHAPTER 3

ABSURD THEOLOGY

Theology is the study of God, how he thinks and acts. It is what a person believes about God. The Bible is our guide to theology. According to it, God has never changed. He is the same God today as he was thousands of years ago. Yet, my absurd religion changes him whenever it wants into whatever it wants. Now we have a variety of Gods: one church has an angry God, another preaches a happy God. Some preach a loving God, others a judgmental God, some a big and powerful God, others a sissy God. My religion isn't beyond giving God an extreme makeover, re-creating him to fit who they have become.

When people tamper with God's character to fit who they are, theology becomes absurd. We can't create a God who loves what we love, hates what we hate and agrees with us on all of our political positions, without becoming absurd. Yet all religions do this— including my own.

I'm tired of having a God who looks like me, smells like me, likes the same TV shows and orders the same flavor of ice cream. I want someone different and better than myself. I want to know the real God, not a mega-me God. I want the same God that Moses and Elijah had. I want the God who Jesus stayed up all night talking to. But absurd theology keeps getting in my way. It won't let me have that God. It keeps telling me that he is now inactive or off-duty.

An Absurd Encounter

There are so many different theologies floating around it is hard to know what this gospel is really all about. Some people believe it's about trying to be good and then going to heaven. They believe Christians should have better than average morals, do good deeds and love other people. But I wonder: Did Jesus really die so we could give a few bucks to the homeless, have impeccable morals, and end up in heaven? Is that the theology of the Bible? Is that why God sent Jesus to earth?

Early in my life as a Christian I began asking good, honest questions like that, but I always bumped into absurd theological answers. I wasn't trying to prove Christianity was wrong. On the contrary, I believed in it and wanted to make my living preaching it. So one day I asked a local "theologian" why God created mankind on earth in the first place. The conversation went something like this:

LOCAL THEOLOGIAN: "God loves you so much, Steve, that he sent his Son Jesus to die for you, so that when you die, you can go to heaven and be with God."

ME: "So God's real intention is to get me into heaven?"

LOCAL THEOLOGIAN: "That's right."

ME: "But if God just wants me to be in heaven with him, then why didn't he just create me up there in the first place? If God loves me so much, why risk losing me in the mess down here? After all, I might decide not to follow Jesus, or I might become a priest of darkness. I might decide to bite the head off a chicken and drink its blood or get a full body tattoo. Then what will happen to me? If God wants me so badly, then why risk losing me to the devil and make me live down here in disease, death, and war?"

LOCAL THEOLOGIAN (aghast): "That's, well ..."

ME: "Besides, don't theologians say that all those who believe in Jesus are someday coming back to earth to rule and reign with him?"

LOCAL THEOLOGIAN: "That's correct."

ME: "So God created me here on earth, but he loves me so much he wants me in heaven with him? But when I get to heaven he's going to send me and millions of others right back to earth again and then do what?"

LOCAL THEOLOGIAN: (makes strange noises) %$#@#$%^

This theologian had no answer. Unfortunately, millions are taught today that this gospel has little to do with our present world. It is all about going somewhere else called heaven and that is that. What I needed back then was some good theology to find out what this gospel is really all about.

The Gospel of Him

The best place to find what this gospel is really all about is, obviously, the Bible. It makes good sense to go to the gospels to define the gospel, don't you think? As you may know if you have some Sunday school background, there are four gospels: Matthew, Mark, Luke and John. Here's a surprise: Mark was actually written first, even though Matthew gets first place in the New Testament. Many scholars believe other writers such as Luke used the book of Mark as a reference to their writing.

When we open the first gospel written, Mark, we don't have to look very far for the answer to our question. The very first line of Mark supplies it: "The beginning of the gospel about Jesus Christ, the Son of God."

In plain English we learn immediately what the gospel is and what it is not. The gospel is about Jesus. It isn't about God loving me. It is not about me loving people. It isn't about getting us all to heaven. No, the first gospel written is about Jesus Christ, the Son of God.

I think I could ask every preacher within a hundred miles of me what the gospel is about and ninety nine percent would get it wrong. I've heard a lot of sermons in my day and have been to hundreds of churches around the world. But I have heard relatively few sermons about Jesus Christ. Plenty of sermons reference Jesus, but the ones I've heard are primarily about our needs, our hurts, and our blessings. They are about us, not him.

To be sure, Jesus did do a lot for us. That's great news, but it's not the primary news. The primary news is about Jesus himself. My absurd religion is like a kid who skips the main meal to get to the dessert. Ministers today are so eager to get to the self-gratifying stuff that most of America thinks the gospel is about Jesus coming to make us happy and fulfilled. Too many churches have become a dessert buffet of inspirational feel-good theology.

" I think I could ask every preacher within a hundred miles of me what the gospel is about and ninety nine percent would get it wrong. "

Wouldn't it be fun to make up a new rule? Let's do it. The new rule says that all preachers, teachers, and religious leaders everywhere are not allowed to preach a sermon on self worth, self image or self love, or even about meeting society's needs, but only about Jesus Christ himself. With a rule like that, many preachers would be left stuttering behind their pulpits.

The Gospel of the Inactive God

Some preachers, as I've said, think the gospel is only about getting into heaven. But to me, the good news is that God will come down from heaven and be with us here, not that we will someday go to heaven. Absurd religion offers a God who lives upstairs and is presently unavailable; but I get to see him after I die. My absurd religion has become so powerless and ineffec-

tive in this life that it has little left to offer but an afterlife. But
the gospels written by Matthew, Mark, Luke and John reveal an
interactive God. They depict a God who did come down from
heaven through his son Jesus. Conceived by God and born of a
young woman named Mary, Jesus became a new kind of human
being the earth had never seen before. His goal was to create
an entire new race of humans. The gospel, then, is about Jesus.
It is about him redefining and recreating a new humanity that
lives on earth so it can interact with God. Yes, we have the
promise of heaven at death, but we also have a lot to do before
we get there.

**" My absurd religion has become so powerless
and ineffective in this life that it has little left to
offer but an afterlife. "**

Jesus, the new kind of human, interacted with God in ways
never known or seen before. This new man Jesus, is actually the
"stop, look and listen" Savior. He had the ability to somehow
stop what he was doing, see into heaven and hear what God
was saying. Through Jesus, God was neither controlling the
world nor abandoning the world. Instead, Jesus interacted with
God while in this world. The application is clear. Jesus went
to heaven after he died. Those on earth who believe in Jesus
follow the same pattern and continue to interact with God in
his place.

Unfortunately, absurd theology has downsized God, changing the powerfully interactive God into a simple inspirational
God. It gives us a God who comforts us in our sorrows and in-
spires us to keep going in spite of them. Inspiring is only a sliver
of God's role towards people. His major activities are to save,
deliver, heal, protect and even step onto the battlefield to fight
for his people. However, you'll not find that active God being
preached at the tidy church on the corner. No. The interactive
God is like a relic, packed away in a musty trunk somewhere in
the church attic.

The Gospel of the Upset God

My absurd theology also believes in the upset God, except He is
always upset with someone else. He is upset with homosexuals,
drug dealers, pornographers, and other flagrantly sinful people.
But I've noticed in the Bible, when God gets upset, it is usually
with his own people! The biggest upsets in history have always
been when his people forsook him, ignored him, or remade him
to fit their own likes and dislikes. In the last book of the Bible,
Revelation, Jesus calls six out of his seven churches to repent—or
else.

Yes, God may be upset, but it's primarily with his own people
who lay claim to him, but have no time or interest in him. If
you examine churches from all denominations, you will see the
same pattern. In judgment, God has simply withdrawn from
their gatherings, leaving beautiful buildings filled with lovely
music and well-dressed people, but without any evidence of his
presence or power. God's problem is that his own people want

their own will and their own way. If he is upset, he is upset with them.

" My absurd theology also believes in the upset God, except He is always upset with someone else. "

The good news is that God is still willing to work through his own people to change the world, if they would turn to him with all of their heart. The book of Acts is replete with accounts of God working through ordinary people, bringing healing, deliverance from demons, and help of all kinds. Why? Because God was interacting with them. Through their own hands and mouths, God was waging war against evil's grip and this is still the way God chooses to fight against darkness today.

The Workers Are Few

Today it is common for churches to send people around the world to evangelize non-believers. The goal is to get people to become a Christian so at death they will go to heaven. Churches also send groups out on good deeds missions to build buildings in Third World countries or to put shoes on the feet of poor children and provide enough money for a meal a day. These may be good things to do, but in all the recorded acts of Jesus, he never did these things.

I am sure there must have been many shoeless kids in Jesus' day, but there are no accounts of him supplying them with any. There must have been hungry children with big round bellies like the ones you see in those TV commercials, but Jesus never raised money to buy them food. He didn't busy the disciples building synagogues for poor Jews or houses for the hundreds who had lost their homes to the Roman tax collectors.

Instead, Jesus cut at the root of evil with the power of God. He went after the demons that kept society corrupt and sick. He freed entire communities from the powers of darkness that held the people in poverty. He cast out the spirit of corruption and taught them the way of love, honesty and generosity.

I took a trip to Guadalajara, Mexico, a few years ago. Guadalajara is a favorite destination for Americans who want to evangelize people, often by handing out gospel pamphlets on street corners. At the airport I saw scattered groups of Americans dressed like carpenters, prepared to spend a week or two hammering together a bare-bones church in some distant village. I thought it was a bit hypocritical since I knew none of these volunteers would ever attend the kind of churches they built with hard wood benches, dirt floors, and no air conditioning.

After checking into the hotel, it seemed like a good time to enjoy the typical Mexican morning. The sun was shining and vendors were selling mangos and bananas. I decided to take a stroll down to the corner and back. What do you think I found? People on every street corner from all over the United States, each with their matching t-shirts, handing out tracts and "witnessing." They were practically running into each other. In fact, sometimes they seemed to be in competition for a "lost soul." Jesus once said the workers were few, but apparently times have changed. This downtown street seemed over-run with Christian workers.

I had brought a group, too, of twenty or so people. We didn't bring anything to hand out. We had no carpenter's tool belts. We weren't there to build a church or feed the poor. Our goal was to help believers encounter the presence of God. I knew then, as I know today, that if anyone experiences the presence of God just as they did in the Bible, his or her life will get better. Eventually they can build their own homes and buy their own food and shoes. Jesus used this pattern, too.

" I knew then, as I know today, that if anyone experiences the presence of God just as they did in the Bible, his or her life will get better."

The diagnosis Jesus gave to his generation was simple: The people living in Israel were harassed and helpless. Building a house, putting shoes on their feet or buying them rice would have only made them more comfortable in their misery. Herein lies the problem then and now. There have always been plenty of do-good workers. The shortage is with the kind of workers Jesus needs who will do what he wants done. Here is what he did: He called his twelve disciples and sent them to drive out evil spirits, heal the sick and announce that the kingdom of God had arrived. We may have our own brand of workers, but where are God's kind of workers? Most churches don't have those kinds. Why? Because my absurd theology has explained the need for them away and doesn't have the faith for them. It thinks we are so advanced with our doctors, psychologists, and modern remedies that we don't need God's help.

I do thank God for doctors, but is it enough? Not by a long shot. Today people face depression, suicide and abuse in epidemic proportions. It isn't safe for our children to play alone in their own yards or feel secure in their own schools. It will take much more than what we can do on our own to save us now. How did Jesus solve the problems of his day? He bypassed the absurd religion and got workers from among ordinary people like Peter, Andrew, James and John to get the job done. These ordinary fishermen may have smelled like a seafood buffet, but at least they weren't blinded by crazy theology.

Don't Even Ask for a Miracle

One of the more damaging absurdities that robs us all is the teaching that miracles are not for today. My absurd religion doesn't deny the Bible miracles of the past. It just believes they will never happen again. It thinks they were only for a certain time, and that time is over. Absurd religion believes that God only used miracles to prove a point. For instance, it teaches that God had to prove that Jesus was real, so he allowed miracles. He also had to prove the Bible writers were real, so they got miracles, too. Now that Jesus has proven himself, and the Bible is written, miracles have ceased. So goes their logic.

I think it is clear when reading the Bible, particularly the Book of Acts, that those writers never thought the day of supernatural events would ever end. Clearly, it wasn't the Apostles doing the miracles anyway; it was the Holy Spirit. Peter said in Acts 2:39 that the Holy Spirit is a gift that comes to every generation, not just one.

This same spirit is available to you and to your children, those far off and everyone whom the Lord calls. This idea of a powerless God really took off when a man named Augustine started writing around 400 AD. Later, after experiencing some miraculous events himself, he retracted some of his statements. In fact, in 428 AD, two years before his death, he completed his final book called "Retractions." But it was too late. His idea that the power of God had ended with the Apostles had already taken root in absurd theology. His original teaching on the cessation of miracles is still the daily bread of many preachers today.

" I think it is clear when reading the Bible, particularly the Book of Acts, that those writers never thought the day of supernatural events would ever end. "

The Value of Good Theology

Winston Churchill wasn't part of the English clergy. But boy could he preach! In my opinion, his "bull dog" speeches saved the British Empire from falling into the hands of the Nazis during World War II. Churchill wasn't a theologian either. Yet, he believed and convinced a nation that it was God's will for them to win the war. Nearly seventy years has passed since World War II, but I am still inspired by Churchill's theology of victory. His words landed harder and lasted longer than Hitler's bombs. Here are the concluding words from the speech delivered June 4, 1940:

> "We shall never surrender and even if, which I do not for the moment believe, this island or a large part of it were subjugated and starving, then our empire beyond the seas, armed and guarded by the British Fleet, will carry on the struggle until in God's good time the New World with all its power and might, sets forth to the liberation and rescue of the Old."

That's the kind of theology that can unite a nation. But in the same way, bad theology will scatter and divide a people. Does my own nation want to believe in a mighty God? I believe it does, but bad theology keeps telling them not to. Something is wrong.

We are in desperate need today of good theology in our churches that promotes the complete God of the Bible. Good scholarship does exist today, but most of it never makes it to the pulpit. Instead, headline theology is standard fare for many preachers. They read the latest newspapers and then squeeze God into the picture.

Part of the problem is my absurd religion wants to control what the Bible says. It controls the Bible's teaching out of the fear of losing control of the people who read it. The Catholics tried to do the same thing centuries ago by translating the Bible into Latin. The common person couldn't read it. They even killed the first man who translated it into English. Today, bad theology controls people by lifting scriptures out of context, time, culture and history. Then, like fitting a square peg into a round hole, it forces the Bible to say whatever it wants. To preserve and protect itself, it has created God in its own image. The God of absurd religion is just like them: powerless, self-centered and upset with everybody else.

Absurd religion can be fixed, but not without some changes. First, we need theology that keeps the Bible in context. Context means interpreting the Bible according to and through the original intended audience. In other words, what did it mean to the people who first heard it spoken or read? It is absurd to skip over the original first century audience and force the Bible to fit our culture two thousand years later.

" Today, bad theology controls people by lifting scriptures out of context, time, culture and history. "

Second, religion must accept responsibility for allowing bad theology to become so popular. America needs someone like Churchill with a "V for Victory" voice to snap us out of our self-destructive tendencies. Finger pointing theology will continue to divide America. But theology becomes good when God speaks for himself, and those who believe it fit themselves into it. Good theology applied is the only way we will ever become the light of the world and have a chance to save our nation from its downward spiral.

Jerry's Story

When I first became a Christian, I thought I really knew the Lord. I could feel his presence and was aware of his will. Everything about him and his purposes for me sprang to life in my heart.

However, when I went to Bible college I was told by my professors that I didn't really know God at all. They said, "You must be trained in the proper theological methods to actually know the Creator of the Universe." Suddenly, the God I had known became distant.

Under their training God became remote and unmoved. Once I believed in his power for healing and provision, but they taught me to believe that God did not involve himself in the small matters of day-to-day life. For me, he had really become the "man upstairs;" a powerful, unknowable father you best not bother.

I embraced a theology that, while claiming to make God clearer, actually made him more confusing. My professors made God out to be the one who actively brought both sickness and healing upon people. They depicted him as the one who oppressed and delivered. In class we were taught to be careful because you never knew when God might decide to strike you down. Sometimes we didn't know whether we should pray for change, or just wait for God's will to come to pass.

In the years that followed, a deeper prayer life and more diligent study of scripture brought a different understanding. I slowly became re-acquainted with the One I first met so many years ago. With his glorious presence and the fellowship of other faithful believers, I learned to see beyond the empty theology I had been taught.

How can I point out that morality is getting more attention than it deserves without sounding like I am promoting immorality? There is more to this religion than morality and we may be missing the best parts.

CHAPTER 4

ABSURD MORALITY

The Ten Commandments are back in the news. Some group was protesting because they had been taken down from the courthouse wall. Another group was protesting so they would not be put back up. A judge will end up deciding. Nobody knows which group will win, and I'm not sure it really matters. If we hang them back up in the courthouse is it really a triumph? Is America a better place for it? I mean, if we read the Ten Commandments to a group of hardened criminals, what outcome should we expect? Would there be an extreme moral makeover right on the spot? I'm leaning toward "no."

However, today, when it comes to these protests about God's commandments, I think I have a better idea of what's going on. I understand and sympathize with those who are genuinely concerned with the moral condition of America. But is it possible that personal morality plays too big a part in our religion? Have we made it the center of our beliefs when it's only a peripheral matter?

Powerless to Change

Let me hit you with a surprising fact. Do you know what the New Testament says about the Ten Commandments? It says they are powerless because of our sinfulness. Without some greater power over our sinfulness, the Commandments alone are ineffective. You can read it for yourself in the New Testament book of Romans, the eighth chapter, verse three. When I read that, a major light bulb went on over my head. The Ten Commandments can point out what God wants of us, but they remain powerless to help us or change us or change our sinful nature. If a judge does decide to approve displaying the Ten Commandments, what do we actually get? We get a legal and emotional victory, but is it a moral one? The clear biblical answer is no.

" But is it possible that personal morality plays too big a part in our religion? "

Personal morality is at the center of my absurd religion, and I think it's out of place there. That's a risky statement because to some it might appear I am promoting immorality in the church, or inventing a weird "do what feels good" religion. But that would miss my point. Of course morality has to have a place in Christianity. But it turns absurd when morality becomes the pivotal center of our view of God.

In another chapter, I mentioned that the guilt-ridden, anxiety driven religion of Martin Luther doesn't work. I think I am safe in saying that Luther's obsession with sin has caused personal morality to remain in the center of the Protestant movement. Religion has become about pushing morality on others. Church becomes a place where moral people practice and promote their morality. Today we have groups and organizations that, like Luther, believe that immorality is the problem and morality the answer. Displaying the commandments in a courthouse or school relieves some of their anxiety and insecurity.

However, trying to create a moral anxiety is not helping America. It is dividing America. Telling people to be moral doesn't work. Passing moral laws may protect the innocent from devious deeds, but it won't create a moral society. Reading, posting, or memorizing the Ten Commandments won't work. Those rules may instruct us, but they are powerless to change us. That's what the Bible itself says.

The Bible promises that God has the power to help us change, but morality without that power is absurd. Yet, many preachers of morality in American religion portray God as powerless today. They teach that God's power to do miracles ended with the Apostles. They don't believe God helps people by doing miracles now. To them, a miracle was God's way of promoting himself until the Bible could be written. Now that we have the Bible, we don't need miracles anymore—or so they say.

For a minister to take the power of God out of the Bible is an absurd idea. It removes any hope we have of changing. Then to turn around and tell the rest of the world they need to be moral is even worse. You can see what it is doing to our country. At the end of the day we have a divided nation that is no more moral than when we started. Efforts to force morality on others just make Christians look foolish.

Here is my idea: God wants to show himself strong, powerful, and mighty in our day, just as he did throughout history. I believe it is his choice for every ordinary person to experience his presence. When I say "his presence" I mean a tangible knowing. A tangible knowing includes things we can see, as well as things we can't see. It can be a feeling or a sense. It is an internal knowing that God is with us, is active in our lives, and cares about us. In fact, I believe everyone's life should include some God events.

" Efforts to force morality on others just make Christians look foolish. "

Why don't most churches have his presence? I think it's because the people who control religion in America have never experienced it. You can't give to others what you don't have. Another reason is that the controllers are embarrassed by outward displays of emotion. They would rather remain safe, reserved, and coddle their people, while at the same time telling the rest of the world to change.

It looks to me like it's up to the ordinary people to demand that we get the God of the Bible back. The present religious system isn't going to do it. We need fresh voices of faith that can lead us to the power of God. The Hawaiian shirted, latte-drinking pastor who denies God's power is taking us down the wrong road. I wouldn't mind if every "self-help" preacher quit and moved to Phoenix to play golf with retired psychologists and new age gurus. I have personally exhausted myself on "how to," "hang in there," and "try harder" sermons, books, and seminars. I don't need one more brochure inviting me to attend a family values conference. What I need is the big God of the Bible to be active in my life. America can no longer afford a powerless religion that promotes a powerless God. We need less preaching about morality and more preaching on how to get God's activity among us.

How to Get Rest

We are not the first generation to face this problem. Jesus faced it when he started preaching. He ran headlong into the powerless morality of the Pharisees. Those Pharisees had a good idea, just like some of the moralists of our day. They wanted to keep Israel clean and moral. There's nothing wrong with that.

But two things went wrong. First, they became corrupt and fell in love with money. Second, their good idea wasn't working. Instead of opening the way to God, their morality became exclusive and locked most of Israel out. They had a morality that was good—without the power of God—much like today. When Jesus came with changes, they fought back rather than give in. Put it all together, and it was a classic case of religion gone moralistic and powerless.

There is a famous saying from the Bible that maybe you have heard. Jesus said, "Come unto me all you who are weary and heavy laden and I will give you rest." Traditionally preachers use this to launch themselves into an evangelistic sermon. They say that if a sinner will come to Jesus, he or she will find rest for a weary soul. By the way, if this is true, why are churches filled with so many restless people? I see few "resting" people and lots of depressed, oppressed, stressed, fearful, and exhausted people. And these are the Christians.

" They had a morality that was good—without the power of God—much like today. "

Back to my point, which is that Jesus wasn't saying, "Come and find rest" to a godless crowd. It wasn't a salvation sermon. He was speaking to a Jewish crowd. These were insiders, the chosen people. Why would Jesus tell them they could find rest from their weariness? What were they tired of? The people of God had completely exhausted themselves trying to be moral Jews under the system of the Pharisees. They needed rest from a moralistic religious system that had become void of the power of God.

Jesus was inviting them to embrace his ministry of proven power. He did not start out by pushing morality. He lightened the load not by lowering the moral standard, but by increasing the presence of God for those around him.

I like what the presence of God does. It pulls people in. It breaks down barriers of race, religion and even morals. It brings successful people and failures together under one banner. When the power of God is present, everyone is having a tangible experience together with the living God. It is a time of knowing God in a way you can feel, but perhaps not explain. I believe this presence, all but lost in religion today, is the stuff that makes heroes. The men and women of the Bible are legends because they were ordinary people doing great things by a power that was not their own.

Morality without offering the presence and power of God is just the opposite. It excludes and divides. Morality alone pushes people away; it won't let them in.

Predestined

Many denominations believe that God predetermines who will go to heaven or hell before a person is even born. This explains to me why there is so much religious snobbery in America. The heaven bunch is the elite, hand picked by God, and everybody else is a divine reject. According to this absurd idea, your eternal fate has already been determined. There is nothing you can do about it. I remember as a young minister trying to encourage people to pray. One woman saw no need for it. She said, "Why should we? Everything is fixed and our prayers won't change it."

I know plenty of people who believe in predestination, but I have never met one who believes he is going to hell. I would love to hear a preacher announce on Sunday morning, "God chose me to go to hell, but I am going to preach to you anyway." To these chosen of God, church means self-improvement without any need for transformation. After all, these people are already in, so why worry? Sunday morning means preaching "blessed assurance" to the chosen few and scoping the audience for more of God's elite.

With so much religious elitism, why is there so much concern for the morality of the rest of America? If people are going to hell anyway, why not just leave them alone to enjoy their sin with the time they have left? The answer may surprise you. Absurd religion is less concerned with converting the immoral, and mostly concerned with keeping America morally clean so God won't bring judgment on our nation. They fear that the unclean, immoral people might make such a mess of things that God will send a plague or famine or a stock market crash. What appears to be a real concern for "lost souls" is nothing more than selfish preservation. When the world doesn't go along, God's elite try to legislate morality to protect their own interests.

" It is absurd, exclusive and self-righteous to view yourself as hand picked while the rest of the world is predestined to hell. "

It is absurd, exclusive and self-righteous to view yourself as hand picked while the rest of the world is predestined to hell. The truth is that choices do matter to God. He told Israel they could choose blessing or cursing. God told them they had a choice. They could choose life or death and so can you. Your future, your life, your fate, none of it is fixed. You can choose heaven or you can choose hell. God doesn't do it for you before you are born.

The Real Mission

I think this was the real mission of Jesus. He said he was sent to the lost house of Israel. How were they lost? Did God not know where they were? No, but good Jews were lost in a corrupt, moralistic religion that had separated them from God. Jesus went to find them.

Consider the familiar story of the Good Samaritan that Jesus told in the Bible. A man on a journey was robbed, beaten and left for dead. A Jewish priest saw him, but passed on the other side of the road. A Jewish teacher of the law saw him and passed by on the other side. Later, a Samaritan walked by and helped him, even to the point of paying for the beaten man's care.

What was Jesus trying to tell them? Most of us believe this story is about doing good deeds. Good deeds are right. But the other lesson is when trouble comes don't expect this moral religion to help. It will walk on the other side of the road, unwilling to dirty its hands and believing you probably got what you deserved.

This is the reason many non-religious people are so angry with Christians. Our current religion with its moral standard is pointing its finger and walking on the other side of the street. The answer is not to drop our moral standard. The answer is for Christianity to become empowered again, as it was in the first century.

Morality is not what Christianity or the Bible is about. Morals-based religion is absurd. It always has been, and it always will be. Rather, Christianity is presence-based religion. It is agreed that we can't throw morality away. If we do, we throw part of

God away. And neither can we throw away the power of God. We need all of who God is. One time I was left in a ditch, so to speak. You've probably been there. It was an ugly time in my life. I despaired of life itself. Turning to God was all I knew to do. But when I turned to the God I had grown up with, it wasn't God at all. I had been taught the moral standards about God, but I did not know much of his power. Because my life was going so badly, I concluded that God was mad at me and wanted nothing to do with me.

" Jesus came to deliver us from a system that is exclusive and hypocritical and preaches morality without lifting a finger to help. "

But God surprised me. One day he came to me in an unexpected way. I experienced the power and presence of God for the first time in my life. It wasn't the God of my Sunday school class. It was the God of the Bible. After twenty years of full-time ministry, I became another person.

I didn't change that day because of guilt or anxiety. I didn't change because I was afraid to die and go to hell. Instead, in the twinkling of an eye, I felt God's presence and power, I didn't become a follower of a moral system—I became a follower of God. Like the Israelites in the wilderness, I wanted to go wherever the fire of his presence goes.

Jesus came to deliver us from a system that is exclusive and hypocritical and preaches morality without lifting a finger to help. Good morality is not what makes a Christian. This should be the best news you've heard in a while. No, the mark of a Christian is the presence of God. Think about it—if morality makes a Christian, then Muslims are better ones that we are. They have a much more strict moral system than Christianity. But morality doesn't make a Christian. Presence does. When God was displeased with the children of Israel in the wilderness, he threatened to take away his presence. I think that is pretty much what has happened to my absurd religion.

It is past time for Christianity to do away with preachers who preach morality and a powerless God. I will never be satisfied with a religion that only cleans the outside of the cup. I want my insides cleaned, too.

Jonathan's Story

I had the opportunity to go on a ministry trip to another town. I thought the music and the preaching was great. It was a good service, and people lingered long after it was over.

I lingered too. It had really been a long day, and I was tired. I decided to find a quiet spot to sit down and catch my breath.

My break was interrupted by a small group of prominent members. They began to share with me all the problems in that church, including the faults of the pastor and especially the faults of the musicians and singers.

One woman in the group evidently had once been on the music worship team, but was no longer a part of it, for a reason she didn't reveal. She went on and on about a divorced lady on the team whose husband had left her for another woman. However, she was still allowed to sing on stage.

I just sat back and asked, "Did the man leave her for another woman?"

"Yes," she said.

"Why does that disqualify her?" I asked. "I'm glad she still has the strength to come to church and worship, even though she is probably embarrassed and wounded."

Finally, the lady questioning me asked my opinion about the guitar player. I told her I thought he played well. She asked me if I thought it was right for the worship leader to allow him to play guitar, even though he still smoked cigarettes. She didn't think he should be allowed, since smoking was an immoral practice and his body was the temple of the Holy Spirit.

"You know," I said, "I never really found anything about smoking in the Bible, but I did read something about gossip."

Then I said, "There are some things worse than smoking and divorce. Gossip and envy ruin this for everybody."

I got my moment of quiet back again as they all slipped away and left me to myself.

This chapter was easy to write. There are many voices speaking out against the selfish "me" generation. Unfortunately, my absurd religion has learned to cash in on it and probably won't stop until the people finally say "whoa."

CHAPTER 5

ABSURD HUMANISM

C hurch signs these days read like a psychiatrist's clip-
board. Every church seems eager to out-do the other in
supporting people's fascination with themselves. They
advertise as "The church that cares about you" or "The church
where your needs are met," and they insist "your opinion matters."

Churches have figured out how to make a bundle of money
off the "me" generation, which is obsessed with itself. They do
big business with their care groups, share groups, home groups
and support groups. It's not what people really need, but it is
what the "me" generation wants. This shouldn't be called the
gospel of Christ; it should be called the gospel all about us.

We should make Sigmund Freud the revered founder and
saint of the gospel all about us. He would have understood our
love for self-analysis. He would have appreciated that sermons
in many churches are now "talk therapy." Talk therapy is the
belief that people get better when they talk about their problems.
Preachers use the pulpit like talk group therapy. The preacher

identifies problems we are all facing and then gives a biblical or inspirational conclusion. The power comes from Sigmund Freud, not Jesus Christ. It's psychotherapy wrapped in scripture.

Consider these common sermon topics preached every week in my absurd religion:

Winning over Depression

Dealing with Stress

Handling Your Fears

Ending Frustrations

Realizing Your Full Potential

" This shouldn't be called the gospel of Christ; it should be called the gospel all about us. "

We teach people how to find themselves, love themselves, and forgive themselves. I was even at a church service where we were told to hug ourselves. Watching grown men put their arms around themselves so disgusted me that I had to close my eyes. There are just some things a grown man should not do—give himself a hug is one of them.

The Commercialized Christ

The gospel all about us has given birth to the commercialized Christ. This is the Jesus that is attractive, always positive, family first minded, and wants to take us back to 1957. I say 1957 because that is the year I saw my first hula-hoop. It was a great year to be alive. It was also the year I stood out in the street with everybody else and looked up, waiting for the Soviet-launched Sputnik to cross the sky. My faithful church-attending family moved out to the new suburbs in town that year. John F. Kennedy landed at the small regional airport to make a speech. We stood at the chain link fence that separated us from a future president and listened, watched and wondered. Everybody had a mom and a dad, or so it seemed. Howdy Doody was on TV, Leave it to Beaver began its first season, and The Ten Commandments with Charlton Heston played downtown at the Fox. Yes, the commercialized Christ must live in 1957, or at least want to take us back to when life was like that.

Of course, not everyone is ready and able to go back to the culture and lifestyle of 1957. American society in the twenty-first century has become dysfunctional and distant from each other. It needs help. Fortunately, at most local churches today, you will find the motivational speaking, positive thinking Jesus, ready to save you and prepare your hearts and minds to go back to a time when the world was a clean place to live. Today's sermon is titled, "Be Positive about Yourself," followed by "Loving Yourself," "Forgiving Yourself," and "Accepting Yourself." Yes, this four part series is called, "It's All About You." After the commercialized Christ, the one we love so much, is finished pumping your self-image, you will be ready to travel back to 1957 when God loved America.

Okay, I know the idea of being taken back in time is silly, but does it ever seem to you that some Evangelicals wished we lived in the '50's? What they have done is create a 1950's lifestyle with a 1950's Jesus. To them these were the good old days before abortions were legal. These were the best days because gays still lived in a closet, moms stayed at home and we prayed everyday at school. Does it get any better than that?

You know I was born in the '50's and, as good as they sound, a lot of us born then didn't turn out so good. We rebelled against our parents, our schools and our government. Whatever felt right was right. Our parents gave us more than they ever had, and we got mad at them. We did the same thing to our kids, and now they are mad at us. Maybe we don't want a religion that is still back in the 1950's. But in most churches that is what you are going to get, a 1950's born Jesus.

" This commercialized Christ is no longer the despised and rejected Messiah of the past. "

Everybody loves this Jesus. This Jesus teaches us to do whatever feels right as long as it doesn't hurt anybody. He is all peace and love. This commercialized Christ is no longer the despised and rejected Messiah of the past. The "feel good" teachings of this Jesus are welcome at Wal-Mart, newsstands and airport bookstores. He has terrible theology, but he does sell. This Jesus is a marketing phenomenon. Thanks Jesus! You are everything I ever wanted in a savior. I finally have a purpose in life, and that purpose is me.

Christians on the Couch

When the concept of the Steve and Kathy Show was in the drawing

board stage, everyone asked me, "Who is your target audience?"
I was new at the TV business and must have talked like a rookie.
"Who's my target audience? Shouldn't everybody in the entire
world be my target audience?" I said.

"No, no," they said. "Is your target audience Christian or
non-Christian?"

That was a tough one to answer because, in reality, Christians
and non-Christians these days are not that different. They all
believe that self-analysis brings understanding, and understanding brings light. They all believe what they choose to believe so
they can feel better about themselves. What's the difference?
Church people may talk differently than people who don't go
to church, but they don't think differently. Everybody is self-
absorbed.

Now, don't get me wrong. I am not opposed to feeling better. Who doesn't want to feel better? What I don't like is that
my absurd religion has capitalized on the self-centeredness of
society to benefit itself. It gives people a deceptive sense of what
Christianity is about. Can you imagine Paul writing an entire
chapter in the Bible on how to deal with depression? I mean,
is God our analyst? Do we stretch out on his couch and talk to
him about our mother? Psychoanalysis has its place, but not in
religion—at least not in the religion called Christianity. It makes
ministers say absurd things from the pulpit.

I remember hearing a kind old preacher talk about how special we all are. He was like a Christian Barney, the purple dino-
saur, singing, "I love you, you love me." The words sounded so
good, but they had no effect. If we're all so special, doesn't that

mean that nobody is special? Who goes to a restaurant, asks for the special and hears, "All our food is special"?

Some people waste a lifetime looking for affirmation, and the church is cashing in. Many of us have a driving need to have someone tell us we are good. We want to hear someone say our desires are good, all of our past decisions and motives were good. What better person to say, "You are a good boy or girl," than God himself? If God is not ready to tell me how good I am, then he will help me improve myself until I become a better me.

" Instead of offering a cure, ministers are feeding the need that keeps the people coming back for more. "

I pulled into an intersection one night and just happened to look over at what was to my left. In the car next to me was a person I knew from church. He looked over at me, too, and we waved at each other. He and I were always joking with each other, so I signaled him to roll down his window while we waited for the light to change.

He looked interested, like I was about to say something important. A second before the light turned green I yelled out the window, "God loves me more than you! He carries my picture in his wallet!" I laughed, the light changed and I drove off. Yep, that's the God my absurd religion believes in. He is the God who carries all of our pictures in his wallet and just can't wait to show us off to the relatives.

Behind all this encouraging talk you won't find real answers. Nevertheless, because needy people want to hear reassuring words they keep coming to church, and they support the ministry that makes them feel better. The system creates a co-dependency. Instead of offering a cure, ministers are feeding the need that keeps the people coming back for more.

Jesus didn't use the language of Freud. When he came face to face with a need his words were often sharp and to the point. He would simply say something like this: Ears be open! Spirit be gone! Be made whole! Jesus allowed no one to stay in a victim mentality. His words cured, delivered, and brought life. Jesus cared deeply for humanity—but he was not a humanist.

Jesus was loving, but strict. He told people to love God with all of their hearts, souls, and strength. Wow! That's different from the stuff we hear today from the pulpits. There is no mention in the Bible about loving yourself or forgiving yourself, or hugging yourself either. How many times have I heard it asked, "How can you forgive others until you first forgive yourself?" That thought may sound good, but it isn't a biblical truth. It simply doesn't exist in God's way of thinking.

When I was a teenager it seemed the world was trying to find itself. Some of my friends quit school and rode off into the sunset on various journeys of self-discovery. But what they called "finding yourself" was really feeding yourself. What started out in the 60's as social upheaval turned out to be self-indulgence with longer hair. In the end it didn't work.

God's formula for life has never changed. To find life, you must lose your life.

Lost and Found

For my part I don't need any more "find yourself, feed yourself, love and forgive yourself" teaching. It's like candy—it tastes good, but it doesn't make me healthy. What I want to know is where are those who have lost their lives only to find them again? Isn't that what the Bible says to do? Shouldn't those people be our spiritual leaders?

Absurd religion has totally failed society in this area. In order to gratify itself, it has fed the public candy, until now even the Christians are sick. I think religion's current sickness is what angers and divides America. Those who don't attend church in our society know the church people are just as sick with self-absorption as everyone else is. And they get angry when a sick group of people tries to tell them what to do.

" None of us can afford to listen to anyone, preacher or otherwise, who encourages self-fixation. "

The only way any of us, religious or not, is going to get well is to be freed from absurd humanism. None of us can afford to listen to anyone, preacher or otherwise, who encourages self-fixation. The Bible takes the center off of us and puts it back on God. Compassion for people is good, but it is not the center of biblical Christianity. When religion puts people's wants, needs, hurts, cares, or anything humanistic at its center, it becomes absurd and no longer effective.

If you want to get spiritually and emotionally healthy God's way, then your spiritual center of gravity must change. We must purposely aim at what Jesus wants and cares about. We follow the pattern and attitude he had while here on earth. Jesus cared for all of humanity. Yet the Bible never says humanity was the center of his life and efforts. Jesus was focused on loving and honoring his Father in heaven. He said he would only do what his Father showed him to do. His selflessness towards God made him a servant to mankind.

Reset Your Pre-sets

Most of us have preset decisions in our lives that no longer require much thought. We never ask ourselves whether we should pay the mortgage or the rent this month, or whether we should eat dinner tonight. We simply do it.

So why, when it comes to religion, is everything always subject to our feelings? Because the humanistic gospel caters to our feelings. Our energy is spent constantly analyzing our feelings and then acting accordingly. What a confusing way to live!

Life works much better when we make decisions that are no longer subject to our feelings. There are some things we should always do, and some things we should never do. For example, a Christian should always go to church, always tithe, always worship, and always nurture the fruit of the Spirit. Why? Because the Bible says to, and Jesus did these same things. Some things we should never do are get cranky, gossip, get bitter or judgmental, or return evil for evil. Those are just a few examples. They aren't based on our feelings. They are part of the pre-set behaviors we adopt when we decide to live like Christians. It's much easier to live by pre-sets than to make decisions based on our shifting feelings or moods. It actually becomes a stress reliever.

When we decide to live our lives out for God, we find ourselves less concerned about our self-esteem and our feelings and getting our needs met. We lose the drive to psychoanalyze our emotions and complete the absurd ritual of "finding ourselves."

" When we decide to live our lives out for God, we find ourselves less concerned about our self-esteem and our feelings and getting our needs met. "

The God-centered life is not a magical occurrence. It is simply a matter of a big desire and a little effort. It's putting aside yourself and starting to think the way God tells you to think. The Bible says, "Let this mind be in you that is in Christ." What does that mean? What kind of mind did Christ have? A big aspect of the mind of Christ is simply duty. Jesus had a sense of duty about doing God's work. His duty pre-set took him all the way to the cross. He was like the highly focused, highly trained person you find in the special forces of the military. Jesus had a sense of honor and duty that is often lost in today's mushy theology.

It would be so refreshing to see a restored sense of honor and duty in churches today. Instead, most churches have been sissified by humanism. Congregations are soft and flabby, with no sense of duty and destiny. Most Christians want to be congratulated when they haven't even lifted a finger. If we do anything good it is only our duty, not some sort of favor to God. Instead of exploring our thoughts and feelings, my religion should see how good it feels to live with a sense of honor, duty, and destiny. Our world is in trouble and needs our help. The only way we can help is to lose ourselves like good soldiers for the sake of the mission.

The more time I spend with people who live their lives with a sense of duty and destiny, the more I see that following Jesus is all about teamwork and getting the job done. It's about honoring God. It's about doing our duty no matter how we feel. The wonderful result is that we actually begin to experience God like never before. He responds to people who are dutiful in their attitudes and actions.

There are people reading this book who have no interest in church, but still have an interest in God. Unfortunately, when they went to church the connection to God never happened. Why not? Probably because when they got there, they met Sigmund Freud disguised as Jesus Christ. They encountered Sigmund's power, but not God's power. That's why I'm writing this book. I believe you can still have a real encounter with the living God.

Why do I believe this so strongly for you? Because it happened to me. I am a minister, a preacher, and a pastor surrounded by the absurdities of religion. Yet, in spite of it all, I made it to God. He helped me. He changed me. He gave me a life.

I had to learn everything about Christianity over again. It sounds crazy, but for most of my ministry I didn't even love God. I didn't know I was supposed to. I thought Christianity was primarily about loving people, but it's not. Truthfully, not until the last ten years or so of my life have I ever put any effort into loving God. I wanted God to love me. I wanted God to help others love me. I wanted God to help me love others. Somehow I had missed the most significant commandment in the Bible: Love God.

I found it so liberating to discover that the universe is not all about me. I don't have to be the special kid or the center of attention. I simply need to love God. Even prayer is not about me. Jesus said, "Pray like this: Father, hallowed, reverenced, and honored is your name." Immediately Jesus shifted attention to God. When you pray, shift your attention away from yourself as well. It's not about you or me; it's about him.

" If God's kingdom and rule is going to come into your life now, then your kingdom and rule must step aside. "

These days I'm not looking for self-worth. I'm not trying to feel special. I don't have to be God's poster child. I am just me, loving God. I have walked away from absurd religion that doesn't work. I'm inviting you to do the same.

It's very simple. If God's kingdom and rule is going to come into your life now, then your kingdom and rule must step aside. This is healthy for you. It is healthy for me. It really comes down to the old, forgotten idea Jesus talked about of "dying to self." That sounds a lot different than self-esteem—and it should. God's way is not through pumping ourselves up; it's through humility and loss of self.

The "me" generation cannot be first anymore. The center must change. It is time for a God centered religion. When that change happens, God's presence will be real rather than rare. We will get the God of the Bible back. We will see the power of God.

Rita's Story

Betty was the overseer of all the support groups in the church that I used to attend. There was a prop-up group for practically everything: teen alcoholics, unmarried women, overeaters, bereaved, abused, single moms, etc. You name it—Betty oversaw a support group for it.

She was also approved by the pastor to conduct free counseling sessions to release people from their past hurts. A system was designed to determine who needed those sessions. If a person asked for prayer too many times for the same reason, he or she was sent to Betty. I guess I asked too many times, so off to Betty I went.

During our meeting she instructed me in a soft, soothing voice, "Close your eyes and turn off your mind." Of course the lights had been dimmed by this time. Then using the same soothing tone, she began to read from what appeared to be her instruction papers. "The Holy Spirit and Jesus are in the room," she said. However, I sensed nothing but a creepy, eerie feeling.

"Go back to your earliest memory of your hurt. Capture the smells, sounds, sights, and the feeling of things." I had to endure this for an hour. "What color is the room you're in?

*What does it smell like? What sounds do you hear?" Then she
asked about my feelings and told me it was okay to feel angry,
hurt, etc. "There is always a root to every problem," she said,
"and God has to reveal to me whatever that root is."*

*My answers were read back to me during the latter part of
the meeting, and then Betty droned on: "Know that the love
of God is there in that hurtful situation. Everything is okay."*

*Finally, she "analyzed" my condition based on my re-
sponses. Her examination determined if I needed to continue
the sessions. But I had my own analysis: I had no intention of
ever going through that foolishness again!*

*Is this the way Jesus ministered? Didn't he just set people
free without the "travelogue" into the past? Can you imagine
Jesus taking a demonized person back to his or her first "de-
mon day"?*

*Many people left that church because of this hideous, hu-
manistic practice—including me.*

Mary's Story

*It was April 2003. My husband, Dave, and I were visiting
our daughter and son-in-law, Sharon and Bill. We looked
forward to seeing them and our grandson again. Dave and I
were especially excited about this visit because Sharon and
Bill had found a church they liked.*

*On Sunday morning we all went to their church. It was
quite large and oddly enough offered a choice of four or five
venues—you could actually select your desired worship setting.
The selections offered an environment for everyone, in the
name of God, to pacify all consciences. It was a sort of spiritual*

Burger King brandishing its "have it your way" theme.

Sharon opted for the site called the Video Café located in a large room. Sets of white lawn-type chairs dotted the area, complemented by matching end tables between the two chairs of each set. There were about one hundred or so casually dressed people in the room.

A vast array of pastries, donuts, and muffins were there to summon us, joined by soft drinks, juices, and a not too shabby selection of flavored coffees. People made their way to and from the spread of goodies as though at some sort of spur-of-the-moment gathering.

One person played a computerized keyboard and tried to get some people to sing. He was not very successful. Dave and I and one other gentleman were the only people visibly trying to worship. In this place, there was no need to worry about what God wanted—he wasn't there in this silly café church.

Finally, the pastor appeared on a large screen wearing a Hawaiian shirt, beads, and shorts. His message wasn't half-bad, but most people were more interested in refilling their plates and cups than in what he had to say. The entire presentation sent a silent message that God is not that important—and the people responded accordingly.

It became clear that this church was all about making people happy at any cost. I don't care about the café. I just want my children and grandchildren to know the life-changing awe-inspiring presence of God that is available today.

Writing this chapter makes me nervous. Hypocrisy is so common and accepted that I am afraid there must be a little of it in all of us. Church leaders at least need to talk about it. Why not? Everybody else in the world does.

CHAPTER 6

ABSURD HYPOCRISY I

Why don't people go to church? What makes millions of Americans stay home? Some of the best minds in America—pollsters and researchers—are hired to answer that question. They survey and chart trends. Maybe they should just knock on someone's door and ask. I believe that if they knocked on any door in any city in America, they would get the same answer. I always get the same answer when I ask people why they don't go to church. Here's what they tell me: "The church is full of hypocrites." I'm a pastor, and I agree with them.

Many churches try to lure people in with cozy seats and coffee bars. Others try with Hollywood-style productions and cool, "hip" pastors. But the people have already spoken and told us what they want. They want the opposite of hypocrisy. They don't want anything superficial. They want the real thing.

I don't think my absurd religion takes hypocrisy seriously enough. It thinks hypocrisy is on the order of a headache; I think it's more like congestive heart failure. Christians tend to think the "I don't like hypocrites" line is an excuse for non-spiritual people to stay in bed on Sunday morning and watch NASCAR or home and garden shows. The only way to find out the truth is to rid our churches of hypocrisy and see what happens.

People are not the only ones who don't like hypocrisy. God has a strong distaste for it, too, according to what the Bible says. He calls hypocrisy "yeast." What is the main thing yeast does? It takes over a lot of dough. A little bit of yeast can make a whole batch of dough rise, change shape, and become something different. God likes good metaphors, so when he saw hypocrisy among his followers, he thought yeast was the best picture of what hypocrisy does. It affects the whole church by silently invading it and changing it from the inside out.

To extend this metaphor with my own silly addition, I'd say the world is crying out for a home-cooked meal made with pure ingredients at God's house. But the church serves synthetic and processed spiritual food—the food of hypocrisy—and gets synthetic results. Call me extreme, but processed pastors, synthetic and plastic, should be put in the same category with embezzlers. Their hypocrisy becomes a thief that steals everything good from all of us. Worst of all, God will not participate if he finds it in our religious recipe. Like Jesus said, "A little bit of yeast takes over a whole batch of dough." And indeed it has.

Don't think I blame pastors alone for the hypocrisy. Churchgoers have embraced hypocrisy like they embrace the latest church fad. I'm certain that some of you reading this don't go to church, and for good reason. You don't want religion that's as cheap, plastic, and synthetic as your lawn furniture. Well, neither do I.

Dualism: It's Greek to Me

Here's how to be a hypocrite: Compartmentalize your life. Divide the spiritual from the material. Be two different people in those two arenas. That's exactly what religion has done, and as a result religion does not allow people to be fully human and to experience God in every area of life. We lead sub-divided lives. Religion has not even allowed us to enjoy. It has put enjoyment in the fleshly category and, therefore, it is evil.

" But dualism has taught us that the spiritual and the material are like oil and water that don't mix. "

Most people don't want to be hypocrites, but they don't always know how to be otherwise. I think hypocrisy is a learned behavior that we got from the ancient Greeks. They came up with this idea called "dualism," which says that the spiritual world is separate from the material world. In Greek philosophy and religion, the physical body is considered evil. Physical pleasures are evil and in a real spiritual person ought to create guilt feelings. Sound familiar? It's an idea that's at home in most churches around the world.

The Hebrews never thought like that. They saw no division between the spiritual and the material. It was all one, all interconnected. There was no such thing as having either spiritual needs or material needs. A person simply had needs.

But the church has gone Greek. Religion teaches us that spirituality is one thing and the material world is another. It keeps them unnaturally separate. For example, what do you think of when you see the words "a spiritual person"? Freeze the image that comes to mind and examine it. You probably pictured someone with a far-away gaze who is lofty, heavenly minded, always in prayer or meditation, and is disengaged from the physical world. You may even have pictured a monk or a hermit, the ultimate "spiritual" persons in religious history because they separated themselves from the world and pursued non-materialistic lives.

Why do we think of spiritual people as otherworldly? There's no biblical reason to think of them that way. But dualism has taught us that the spiritual and the material are like oil and water that don't mix.

Here's another example: The Greeks gave us the idea of "blessing the food." Since food came from the cursed earth, it needed to be blessed or made pure. The purpose was to change something material and unholy—the food—into something spiritual and holy through prayer. We have to pray for it to become acceptable.

Hebrew thinking, on the other hand, teaches us to bless God, not the food. The Israelites did not pray over their food to bless it; to them it was already blessed. Rather, they held the food before them and blessed the Lord saying, "Blessed are you, Lord our God, King of the universe, who brings forth bread from the earth." They did not classify food as evil or fleshly. They were not dualistic. To them the spirit, the material, the soul, the body, and the flesh were all God's creation, all connected, all good, and meant to be enjoyed.

The dualistic mindset affects the way all of us try to solve the world's problems. Notice that few people in our society run to church when they have material problems. They may occasionally pray and yet still believe that God wants nothing to do with their material everyday needs. To most, church is for inspiration and far removed from the material side of life.

" Everything that happens in life is both material and spiritual because that's the very nature of our existence. "

Some enlightened churches have tried to break out of this dualism—ironically by becoming more aggressively dualistic. They try to meet both spiritual and material needs, but they still keep them separate. To deal with material problems these churches (like many churches through history) become more humanitarian. They operate soup kitchens, orphanages, and charities. They maintain the wall between spiritual and material, but try to succeed in both arenas by doing good deeds. They still see the deeds as essentially material, so when they get back to church they talk otherworldly again. They never make the connection that meeting someone's material needs is a spiritual act, and there really is no separation between the two.

When you start thinking like the Hebrews did, instead of dualistically, it changes your whole worldview—even how you watch the news. TV quickly brings the world's problems into our homes with reports of genocides, storms, famines, and other such disasters affecting humans. But few churchgoers watch the news and see these as spiritual problems with spiritual answers that can change our material world. At most they see them as material—natural problems that spiritual people might help solve with some humanitarian aid or comfort.

The Hebrews made no such separation. When threatened with war, the Hebrews got together and began to call on the name of the Lord. If famine struck they saw it connected as much to the spiritual realm as to the natural. Everything that happens in life is both material and spiritual because that's the very nature of our existence.

Feeling God

What happens when we no longer allow a separation between our spiritual and material selves? What happens when we tear down the walls that compartmentalize us? Something amazing takes place—our lives become three-dimensional and real. We begin to experience God not just as an abstract reality in the spiritual realm, but also as an ever-present being in all of life. We experience God in the real world—at work, in our emotions, in our bodies, in our homes, and in our relationships. We feel energized. Our bodies are not profane, and there's no need to be spiritual only at church.

Real faith is not just mental belief. It is the conviction that God is ready to be active in every sphere of our lives. He is not a compartmentalized God. When God comes into your life, he makes you totally human. He energizes you until you are living life fully. You experience the best that a human can experience because God is at your side in everything.

To be spiritual is to be able to show the world that God is right here, right now. Not by doing humanitarian aid, or going away and writing a book about the visions you had all day long on a mountain top in some remote region of the world. The person truly alive in God brings him into every situation. It's neither the lofty monk nor the soup kitchen person who is being spiritual. It's the person who can see the need, and the disaster, and the relationship—see every situation—and bring God into it.

To be spiritual means to become fully human. It means to feel the restoring power of God in you, and to live as a complete human being with nothing missing. You live uninhibited on the inside without the hindrances, hang-ups, unforgiveness, bitterness, agendas, suspicions, or any of the heavy burdens that can so easily become a part of being human. That's what the Hebrews would call a spiritual person.

I want to live every moment as a whole person. I don't want to be two people residing in the same body. I don't want to be sub-divided. I want to be personally unified. How about you?

I am feeling more confident on the subject of hypocrisy. Religion has become such an "act," an act that I don't think I am a part of. A good image is important, but what we need is a real one without all the fluff and glitter.

CHAPTER 7

ABSURD HYPOCRISY II

Nowhere is hypocrisy more evident in the church than when we talk about money. Blame the love of it, lack of it, want of it, or need of it, but the desire for money now has many churches by the rudder. When money steers the ship, it turns authentic Christianity into a ship of fools. Yet money is the driving force behind most of religion.

The Bible says the love of money is the root of all kinds of evil, and I don't think any one of us would doubt that. You don't even have to believe in God to see that where there is a love for money, every kind of evil pops up and resides there, too. This can happen to rich and poor alike. People who don't have a dime still love money. Poor people can love money just as much as the rich do; they just have less of it to love.

Is money itself evil? No. Can the church survive without money? No. Money is a legitimate need. It can be a wonderful tool. Without money, churches fail. I watched amazed recently as the young pastor of a church I was visiting sat with me in his tiny church office. The books and bookcases on the wall framed

him like an Olin Mills portrait. Tearfully, he poured out his
heart concerning the church's finances. They were in big debt.
They were behind in their building payments. They couldn't pay
their employees' salaries and were two months behind in utilities. Desperately he said, "I don't know what I am going to do. If
there is anything you can do to help, I would greatly appreciate
it."

Money does matter. It mattered to that pastor, and it should
matter to every person who wants God's work to continue. The
question is this: How much should it matter? Some church leaders try to pretend that money does not matter to them at all and
that money is the farthest thing from their minds. But that's a
lie, and it creates a dark place in their hearts where the truth
does not shine, and the love of money grows in secret.

**" Some church leaders try to pretend that money
does not matter to them at all and that money is
the farthest thing from their minds. "**

I was a pretender about money once. When I was 17, I was
so poor that I begged for food from other students during school
lunch. Why didn't I apply for the free school lunch program? I
don't know. I could have. I sure was hungry every day at lunch-
time. When my father died, my mother at first didn't have a job
or even a driver's license. She began working hard every day, and
I didn't want her to know there wasn't enough. My brother got
the lunch money that year. I walked from table to table asking

for food that nobody wanted. Every afternoon I went home and pretended to feel full.

I wasn't a Christian then. I didn't have God's help, and I didn't seek it. I was on my own, trying to make life work. But when I met God, I stopped pretending. The weight of false living was lifted from me. Since then, in both ministry and life in general, I have been open about what I need to live.

That young pastor who was having such financial trouble at his church is a perfect example of the kind of hypocrisy so common today. Later that evening I sat on the front row of his church and watched him perform like a paid actor. He was all smiles. Very upbeat. After a few songs, it was time for the offering. He showed no concern or worry at all, but said, "Folks, this ministry has never been about money, and it never will be. That's why we don't pass the plate around here. In the back of the church is a little box. Just put in what you can, and if you can't, we'll trust in the Lord anyway."

In the space of a few hours he had transformed himself from a legitimately needy ministry leader into a hypocritical fool. His entire conversation that afternoon had been about money. We had knelt and prayed together about money. He had called his banker to borrow more money. Yet, when he got up in front of the people, he appeared as a humble servant with no thought for silver or gold. He may not have been talking about money from the pulpit, but during the week that was all he talked about. And he was hoping to get some money from me that would enable him to continue his masquerade.

I can't afford to live two lives, one in front of my congregation and one in the backrooms. I know I have a responsibility to get people to support what our church does. Here's how I do it: I talk about money. I talk about why we give and how blessed it is to give. My beliefs and my experience have taught me that giving people are the most blessed people on earth.

" My suggestion is for churches everywhere to get real about money, and stop the false humility. "

Once in a great while a visitor to our church misunderstands these "money" talks. They have been wrongly taught that to talk about money is not spiritual. But Jesus talked about money openly. So do I. I tell my congregation how much things cost. Together we give and keep the ministry debt free. In more than twenty years of being a pastor, our church has only borrowed money from a bank one time, and I didn't like it one bit.

My suggestion is for churches everywhere to get real about money, and stop the false humility. It leads to absurd hypocrisy. It cuts off the blessing of God. Remember the yeast Jesus warned about—the yeast of the Pharisees, which is hypocrisy. They loved money, but pretended not to. That was one of their big problems. As for you, talk about money. But don't love it. Keep it in the light; hypocrisy only grows in the dark.

Image Games

Money isn't the only problem that makes churches hypocritical. Church folks love image making and titles. Have you ever noticed that churches can't just do puppets for children—they have to have a puppet ministry? It's not good enough to dress up like a clown and make people laugh. It has to become a clown ministry. This image-making and power posturing is often the worst in small churches that depend on novices and volunteers. Give some people a title, and they want to take over the world.

Image building can create hypocrisy just as easily as money can. Yet some churches are all about projecting the right image to the community, hiding who they really are. This can get them into trouble. They don't want a dinky church building in some forgotten corner of town. They want the big, new-looking structure that makes everyone say "wow" when they drive by. The modern motto for many churches comes right from the *Field of Dreams*. In the movie they say, "If you build it, he will come." The image builders' twist on it is: "If you build it, they will come." Rather than strive to draw the presence of God, which is supposed to be the main purpose, they erect new buildings to attract more people. Yet this image making is costly because big buildings create big debt. The debt requires a church to get people to pay for the building.

The first problem with building a church you can't afford is that it creates a false image of success. It is like someone working for minimum wage buying a fancy sports car and using his entire paycheck to pay for it every month. This person can drive down the street with the top down and people think, "Hey, there goes a success." In reality, he can hardly afford to fill the gas tank. It is hypocrisy from the get-go. In the same way, even if people are attracted to new church buildings, they are being drawn in on false pretenses. What exists in reality is only the appearance of success.

I know of a church group that did this, and their story is painfully instructive. The minister was tired of feeling small. He got tired of his ministry looking insignificant. He searched out a nice piece of property on the new side of town. Another pastor told him about an architect he could hire on the cheap. The church put their old building up for collateral along with whatever bonds, savings, or certificates they had. The small congregation felt so blessed. The bank offered an interest-only loan.

" The first problem with building a church you can't afford is that it creates a false image of success. "

The new building was built on a great location. The pastor could now walk with his head high whenever he was introduced as the pastor of that "new" church. And new people did come. At least some did.

But after a short while, the finance committee got worried. The congregation was struggling to even pay the interest on the loan. The committee called a special meeting with the pastor. They all agreed something needed to be done to attract more people. One man on the committee suggested that the pastor could become a little more "upbeat," more modern. The idea was floated to have a coffee bar before each service. Another man suggested that ending the services as close to noon as possible on Sundays was a good idea. Next, the committee went into a long discussion about their current music director. They wanted someone younger and more exciting.

During the next week they put their plans into motion. The coffee committee was formed. The pastor studied hard that week. He was determined to become more attractive in his preaching. He read an article on the Internet that said references to hell, money, or holiness could make some people uncomfortable, so he decided to leave those words out of his sermons.

When they gave the music director the ax, he didn't take it as well as the finance committee had hoped. He left angrily and took two families with him. The church was now down by two households. For the next few weeks the services went all right. Some members were beginning to feel that the sermons were becoming shallow. They missed the passion of the pastor's old sermons. After a while, three more families left. Now they were down by five families.

Five families leaving with their money put an even heavier burden on the finance committee to make the payments. They called a special meeting of the official church board. One man reminded them of how important it was for everyone to do what was best for the Kingdom of God—even the pastor. So, they decided to consider someone younger, more able to draw in families with children. The need for a successful image took over the church, and when the church didn't grow, the pastor who started it all fell victim to it. He became the scapegoat and ended up without a job.

The story I told you is not an exaggerated account of some church in a far away place. In fact, it is being played out every day in one form or another in cities all over America. It is absurd. It is caused by hypocritical image making.

Inauthentic Authenticity

It's even worse when churches try to create an image of being real without actually getting real with the people. They hire a "cool" preacher with a hip sensibility. A cool preacher gives people hope that they are not stuck in dead religion after all. What says "in touch" better than a preacher in jeans with his shirttail hanging out, or one in khaki shorts with a latte on the pulpit? It is all very deceptive. It's that old time hypocrisy in a better disguise.

" Being more sensitive is strictly a marketing scheme, an image upgrade to grow bigger churches. "

Some churches even make a business decision to become more sensitive to people. I'm all for being sensitive. But does this change in approach mean America has suddenly been flooded with more truly sensitive, caring pastors and leaders? I doubt it. Being more sensitive is strictly a marketing scheme, an image upgrade to grow bigger churches. The only things the church leaders are more sensitive to are growth and money. It is the latest trend to create success for ministries, which is not necessarily success with God for the people in the pews.

Shortening the services, offering coffee bars, encouraging casual dress, and removing references to commitment, sacrifice, or the supernatural power of God are nothing more than marketing strategies. Are people's lives getting better? I don't think so. Time will tell. But from my perspective, church leaders of America are selling their souls in order to "super size." And it's creating more hypocrisy.

Sometimes I wonder: Where are the voices that can call down fire from heaven? Where are the honest, transparent, powerful leaders—not the sensitive sissies following the church's latest marketing plan? Is it possible that God is calling dynamic people with strong convictions and faith to remake what it means to be a Christian? Is it possible to return to the things that actually work? Jesus didn't seem to have a problem attracting crowds.

Get Real With God

In 1995 my life pretty much came to a halt. It seemed as though I was reaping every mistake I had ever made since going into the ministry. There were people in the church that, no matter what I did, were unhappy with me. My wife, Kathy, and I had been married almost twenty years, and I guess we were beginning to show some wear and tear, too. Spiritually I felt as though I had not lived up to what God expected of me. I was trying to be God's man of faith and power, a good husband and a good father, but it was all caving in.

One night I stepped into the garage of our house and just stood there in the dark. I felt like I was at the bottom of a well looking up. It was time for me to get honest. Maybe for the first time, I talked real to God. It was a different kind of talk. I stopped trying to get God to understand how I felt. I stopped

using King James English with "thee's and thou's" to sound spiritual. I talked plainly about who and what I had become. It wasn't
"probably" my fault anymore. It was surely all my fault—and I
told him so. I was the cause of who I had become.

" I had given my own self-image a bare-knuckled beating with the truth—and God liked it. "

Standing in the dark in a garage that reeked of gas and oil,
I told God the truth about me. I didn't leave anything in the
shadows. Suddenly, into that smelly garage, I felt the love of
God come towards me. I don't know how to describe it, but I felt
something. It felt great and so refreshing. I had given my own
self-image a bare-knuckled beating with the truth—and God
liked it. He liked the honesty and transparency. My utter help-
lessness had somehow become more attractive to my heavenly
father than any self-assurance that I would somehow get it all
together soon. His love for me filled that old garage, and I have
never forgotten what it felt like.

That's why today, in a world of absurd religion, hypocritical
love of money and image making, I vote for honesty. Talking
honestly in front of the entire church is freeing. Sure it's risky.
People can leave any time they want. But I think it is the "real"
that keeps them in my church. In fact, I encourage everyone to
get honest before God and each other. Don't get me wrong—I'm
not talking about "tell me how you really feel" therapy. We don't

need to get honest with how we *feel*. We need to get honest with who and what we are, without any excuses.

How to Be You

Recently I was invited to a large church to speak for three days. Everyone was attentive and kind to me, which was somewhat surprising because I said some blunt things to them. I said some of the frank things I am saying in this book. However, on the last day, everyone was extra complimentary. I heard the same compliment repeatedly from the young, old, teenagers, and church leaders. "You're so different," they told me. I heard it so many times that it almost gave me a complex. What kind of weirdo did they see me as? Finally, I stopped the next person that said it and asked, "What do you mean different?" The response changed my life forever.

"You are so transparent and real," was the reply. Transparent and real. Imagine that. I had done nothing special or unique. I hadn't sold them an image. Yet, at the end of each service, hundreds came and asked me to pray for them. And I knew why after hearing their comments. Take me or leave me, I was being me. That's it. I was just being me, and they called it different. My question became this: what were they getting from everybody else? You guessed it. They were getting image making, business decisions, and religious marketing. They had not been getting real. When they saw absurd-less religion, they wanted it.

Let me turn the question to you. Can you be honest with God? I hope after reading this book, you realize you can. We are failing ourselves if we have learned to appear successful when we are not. Of course everybody wants to feel loved. But how much greater is that feeling when you know people are in love with the real "you"—not the super-sized, super-sensitive super-saint you that doesn't really exist.

I hope you see by now that hypocrisy in religion, under any guise, makes no sense. It is absurd. It is everything that Jesus is not. Whoever you are, whether you attend a church or not, the real you wants to be born. You are your greatest selling point. Your successes and your failures are what make you interesting to other people. In fact, those are the things that make you interesting to God, too.

" I hope you see by now that hypocrisy in religion, under any guise, makes no sense. "

One time I asked a very talented young man to speak in one of our services. He was smart and good-looking. He wanted to be a pastor some day, just like me. When he got up to speak he used all of the right scriptures and references. He had done his homework and written a good outline. There was nothing wrong with his introduction or conclusion. He put together a neat, scholarly sermon. But it was awful. It could hardly have been worse. He had left out the main ingredient—the "you."

When he finished he looked pretty downcast. I guess he knew it hadn't gone over that well. He walked over to me with a "what happened" look on his face. And this is what I told him: "I asked you to speak, but you left you out. Your presentation was organized and informative. But I already knew everything you said. Every scripture I had heard before."

He looked puzzled. "So why did you ask me to speak if I didn't have anything to say that you hadn't heard before?" My reply was, "I have heard it all before, but I have never heard *you* say it."

That's the antidote to hypocrisy, my friend. It will make you a success with God, and it will make you a success in life. You don't have to pretend to be something you are not. When you stop being a hypocrite, I can almost guarantee that people will still love you. They will probably love you more. And it will be easier and quicker for you to change because there won't be any more pretending.

Sophie's Story

After driving our younger daughter to a Bible college in Florida, my husband and I seriously considered a move there. We connected with a husband and wife team of Christian realtors and quickly became friends.

They opened their home to us and the following Sunday morning introduced us to their church. It was a massive structure built in the round. The parking lot was so immense that at first we could not find our way out!

Once inside I saw several huge screens and a nicely inclined floor that caused every seat in the house to be a good one. A quick calculation of the lifestyle of our hosts, the attire of the church people, the cars on the parking lot, and the building itself equated to a wealthy church body.

The appearance was one of a spiritual Disney World. Everything seemed to be picture perfect. Later, I found out that this church was under tremendous financial strain. Apparently, the lure to look successful had caused them to build beyond their means. The service was pitched to us with sunny smiles. No one would have guessed there was turmoil behind it all.

Looks were deceiving. The pastor and staff were obviously trained professionals at presenting the "success" image.

The masquerade didn't last. The truth somehow got out to the congregation and the church split in two. One-half left and started another church on the other side of town.

This story is sad, but unfortunately not that rare. There was one thing, though, that made me laugh. The new church that split from the old one was called "Victory." Let the charade begin.

Peoples' fear of authority makes this chapter tricky to write. Down deep I think they want good leaders, but their fears hold them back from fully giving over the reins. Rebellion is so rampant in religion that most churches don't need a pastor; they need a referee.

CHAPTER 8

ABSURD GOVERNMENT

mericans love to be the chief, the head honcho, the top dog. Each of us secretly wants to rule the world. None of us likes being told what to do. Perhaps it goes back to the birth of our country. The United States was birthed in rebellion. We got rid of the English king. The mob won and we've been promoting borderline mob rule ever since.

Is it any surprise that this anti-king attitude would spark an anti-king religion in this country? The problem is God's kingdom isn't subject to mutiny. There is no mob rule. Jesus is the king. He rules. That's that.

My absurd religion seems to think God's anti-democratic style doesn't suit the modern world. They're waiting for God to come around to our way of thinking. They want him to rule through all of us. So, churches set up "democratic" power structures to empower the congregation to control their leaders. But in many cases the democracy turns mob-like very quickly.

The congregation may elect a leader or a preacher, but then won't free him or her to do the job. They continue to vote on every penny spent. They vote on how long the sermon should be each week. They vote on whether or not the pastor should dress up or dress down. The loudest, rudest, meanest, or richest people rule. All is fair in love, war, and church government. The gloves are ripped off, and the brawl is on. The Ultimate Fighting Championship has nothing on this lying, gossiping, backbiting, and backstabbing bunch that rules like the underworld in the local church.

" My absurd religion seems to think God's anti-democratic style doesn't suit the modern world. "

I know of one church that voted that the tithe be changed to five percent. Fancy that! Tithe means ten, and no amount of voting can make it five. But they made it five, and they did it democratically—which is what counts, right? Another church split because someone bought a trash can without taking a vote first. Half the church left and started another church, presumably with the trash can.

I learned the hard way about mob rule. It was during my first year of ministry. Every Sunday at twelve o'clock sharp, a woman would get up during my sermon, go stand at the back door, announce what she thought of my talk, and walk out. It was very disrupting. But I would always say something like, "Thanks for your comments," and then go on with my sermon.

But one Sunday I thought, "Who does this woman think she is?" I got up my nerve and waited. Sure enough, twelve sharp, there she was. This time I interrupted her and kindly asked her to stop. By the reaction I got from some people in the church, you'd have thought I'd asked her to drink poison. That very afternoon the mob took over, mostly by telephone. By the end of the day, I'd been painted as a monster who'd viciously gone after a sweet little old lady. Part of the mob left the church, and part of it stayed. But the part that left was far from done.

Rumors began to spread throughout the town. The school, the post office and of course, the church were all buzzing. The mob made up a piece of pure fiction that after the service started I locked the church door so people could not get out. The same door that opened so easily every week for that woman was now the door that supposedly had been locked, turning everyone into helpless prisoners. That rumor got started more than twenty years ago, but if you go to that town today, they still refer to me as the pastor who used to lock the church door.

This was how the mob ruled the church I was in. They practiced their form of religious wickedness and then would turn right around and preach morality to the world.

One vs. the Mob

Mobs like this rule churches and their leaders all over the world. You see, usually a pastor or minister is offered more than just a job and a paycheck. They get an entire package. Most of the time, the package includes a furnished home or parsonage with all the utilities paid for by the church. Also included might be a car allowance, health benefits, life insurance and retirement. At first glance it looks like a smooth deal, huh?

Think of it another way. If something goes wrong (and it will), the minister loses not just a job, but everything else too. Now how bold, honest and truthful is the "man of God" going to be when the people who can fire him are sitting in the congregation? No wonder the most that people get from their church is an inspirational talk and a pat on the back. These pastors are owned by the mob and paid off by the mob. My absurd religion is a breeding ground for cowards in a world that desperately needs heroes.

Recently I heard a well-known news commentator say, "Where are the pastors? Where are the ministers?" He was hoping for a voice to come forth to help set our nation right. He was wishing for heroes in an absurd religion that is set up to create non-heroes who just go along with the system.

God's government is different from church mob rule. His government is supposed to be God-ruled. But God is invisible. Consequently, He must work through visible people. I've looked at the history of God-chosen leaders and noticed that God never starts with a mob. He always starts with one person. When God wanted to form a group of people, he chose an individual, Abraham, to work through. Abraham, the individual, then became the nation of Israel. Later, when God heard the cries of Israel in slavery to Pharaoh, he chose Moses to be the leader who would set his people free. That's how God works. The greatest need of my absurd religion is not new ideas, but new leaders—God's kind of leaders and churches that will allow them to lead.

As it is, my absurd religion only works for those who have learned to work the system. Behind most pulpits is a politician who has learned to bend with the mob and the money. Today we have politically correct politicians in pulpits across America who must win the vote of the people if they want to keep their job. I would love to see modern day apostles emerge to lead people, but in the present situation, a person with the soul of a biblical apostle would be viewed with suspicion and fear. The news media hasn't helped. It has heightened our fears of strong leaders by spotlighting cultists, charlatans, and crooks.

" The greatest need of my absurd religion is not new ideas, but new leaders. "

We all know there are some bad leaders out there. There will always be a few dictators, those who rule big and live high off a subservient congregation. But is that the norm in my absurd religion? In America eighty percent of our churches number under two hundred people. A board rules the majority of those eighty percent and the minister is only a hireling listening to men in business suits rather than God.

What America has earned for itself is a generation of pastors who are beaten down, afraid of offending, eager to please, and insecure. They have no strength with which to fight the mob or the money. Inwardly they hunger for truth and the presence of the living God, but absurd religion won't let them have either.

Calling All Leaders

I was a mob-ruled leader myself until one day I decided that I wouldn't appease the mob anymore. I wanted my life back, and

I wanted to have God, too. On March 10, 1996, I walked out of my church after twelve years. During the next two weeks, I walked through what I would call "the valley of the shadow of death." It was a horrible time of soul-searching, but in the process I found my life, and I found my God. I decided I would never be ruled by fear of the mob again. I would never put on my religion like a show to please the people. I would be me. I would sound and act like me. If God could use me, then I would be a blessed man. If my absurd religion didn't want me, what would I lose? Nothing.

" Democracy is not the way God gets things done. "

Historically the church has been the earthly power that changes the world. The problem is God will never use mob rule. He will always pick one person. Then that person will reach a group, and that group will reach a community and perhaps even touch the nations. We desperately need religion to take its rightful place in society. We need new leaders, but they will only arise when congregations allow God to give us the kind of men and women we need. Democracy is not the way God gets things done.

My absurd religion must be delivered from its absurd governmental ways that would rather overthrow its leaders than be ruled by His chosen men and women. Let's have another revolution—against mob rule and for the rule of God. It may sound risky, but it's the only sure way to be free of absurd religion.

Ben's Story

As a young, inexperienced and naïve believer, I was asked to pastor a small church. I should have seen the problems coming when I was introduced to the board of elders. At the time there were about 35 to 40 members in the church including children, and there were nine elders on the governing board. They did agree that they wanted me to be the "pastor." What I didn't know was how they were defining pastor.

The words of Jesus in the gospel of John, chapter 10, have a special significance for me. Jesus is discussing sheep, shepherds and hirelings. I thought this church wanted a shepherd. What they really wanted was a hireling, a hired hand. In their minds it was their church and their flock. I worked for them, but wasn't accepted as an equal with them.

As time passed I tried to work within their system, but it failed. There was a continual contention and fight for whose leadership and what vision and direction the church should take. I would spend my days praying and seeking the will of God, and then have to deal with the opinions of these men who were out doing business all day, never giving God a thought. They made me a hireling and put me in an impossible position that was destined to fail.

After working for 15 years in this contentious and draining situation, trying to care for and lead the congregation, I began to seek more of God. I was looking for help, for change, for the power of God, for a true revival and transformation in the

church. This brought all the differences with the board to a
head, and the elders finally asked me to step down.

I took my family to a church where God's presence was so
real that it felt like he was right there in the room with me.
While there God healed my broken heart, gave me hope, and
changed me into a new person. He rescued my wife, my family, and our future. New ministry opened before us.

Now I serve as part of a pastoral team that cares for a
large congregation. Our senior pastor actually leads the team
and the congregation. Since joining the team eight years ago,
I can truly say it is a joy to pastor and serve.

I wonder if a chapter on women will make me a hero with my wife. The subject is too big for one chapter. It deserves an extra book. Maybe this will get somebody pointed in the right direction.

CHAPTER 9

ABSURD PREJUDICE—WOMEN

"God created Adam master and lord of living creatures, but Eve spoilt all, when she persuaded him to set himself above God's will. 'Tis you women, with your tricks and artifices, that lead men into error."

\- Martin Luther

The other day I was handed an article titled, "What about women?" It was written by a Christian author. My first thought was, "What about women?" Hasn't this been settled already?

It appears that the church worldwide still doesn't know what to do with women, and that has created an absurd prejudice within our ranks. My wife, Kathy, has always ministered right alongside me. We have rarely encountered problems with this. One man, after a particular service, angrily said to me, "I don't believe in the ordination of women." I asked him, "So you believe in their subordination?" He didn't answer. It was a great moment.

Perhaps the word "subordination" sounds a little harsh, but isn't that what the "woman question" is really about? Will we as Christians place women in subordination to men? Is this what God intends? I can already tell you that God isn't very keen on subordinating any human being to another.

What Scripture Really Says About Women

Still there are those nagging scriptures in the New Testament about submission and keeping women silent in the church. Yes, those scriptures do exist, but to get their real meaning we must stop letting our prejudices and cultural ignorance guide us.

Let me illustrate with a real story. Some years ago I was in a meeting of men only. We were going to discuss certain policies of the church that would affect us all. As the meeting was about to start, I noticed all of our wives sitting in the hallway outside. I suggested that we bring them in so we could work out the policies together. The men agreed, but it turned out to be a bad idea.

" I can already tell you that God isn't very keen on subordinating any human being to another. "

The women hadn't been involved until that night and they had no idea what had been discussed previously. The entire first hour was spent with the women asking questions and wanting more information to be sure they were clear on every issue. There was nothing wrong with that, but we only had that night to make a decision. We weren't moving forward.

Finally I had to institute a new "rule." I asked our ladies not to ask questions anymore, at least until they got home. It wasn't because they were women. It was because they were new to the proceedings. We then made the best decision that time allowed. Now let me ask you this: Does that mean I have a problem with women? After all I had made a rule that effectively shut them up. Was my rule meant to govern my church for the rest of its existence? The answer is no. The rule was not based on prejudice, but on circumstances. The circumstances made the rule of no talking or asking questions necessary. The rule would only apply again if that group was ever in those same circumstances again.

The apostle Paul made a rule one time, too. He said he didn't allow women to speak in church. Was Paul against women ministers? Did he believe that God wanted women to be subordinate to men? Many men and women think so to this day. They think Paul's rule was God's rule for all time.

But why did Paul require women to be silent in church in the first place? Because the women in Paul's day were generally uneducated. Most of them had never even been allowed to participate in church services or other important meetings. To those women church was a strange place with strange practices. They simply didn't understand what they were seeing or hearing. Many had just recently come out of pagan religion. So during church services their curiosity and wonder got the best of them. They spoke aloud. They asked questions. This soon became disruptive. So Paul made a rule—not a commandment that lasted forever, but a circumstantial rule: "Hey girls, ask your questions at home."

It's that simple. It wasn't God giving orders about women not ministering. It was Paul being organized. In reality, this was a historic moment for women. Sure they had to be silent. But only because they were not yet knowledgeable enough to speak. Paul was actually allowing women, who were considered by many to be second-class citizens, into the church. He was letting them in and allowing them to learn. This guy was for women's liberation long before the National Organization of Women.

Absurd Home Life

When people miss the point of these passages it creates crazy behavior at church and in the home. Here's an example of what I mean: A young couple made an appointment with me for marriage counseling. They were fighting every day and wanted help. I had never met them before, but listened politely to their story.

It seems the young man had been out drinking with his buddies the night before. After he came home, he and his wife began to fight over something silly. During a heated moment she yelled, "I don't have to listen to you." The drunken husband yelled back, "Oh yes you do. The Bible says the wife is supposed to submit to the husband."

This scenario may seem absurd, but it happens every day. Here's a guy who hadn't been to Sunday school since the fourth grade, trying to use the Bible to win an argument. First, let's end the foolishness. The Bible is not available to be used by anyone at any time. If you don't live the Bible everyday, you become disqualified to use it for special purposes—in this case as a weapon. Second, if a person doesn't believe and apply the entire Bible, they become disqualified to use even a small part of it.

The idea that every married man is the head of his wife just because he is a man is absurd. God will never put an idiot in charge of anything. Women never have to submit to a man because he is a man. You only submit to a man because he is a leader. God never intended a wife to submit to a husband's whims and wants. A husband doesn't just get to watch whatever he wants on TV while his wife sits by patiently, putting up with whatever program he chooses.

" If you don't live the Bible everyday, you become disqualified to use it for special purposes—in this case as a weapon. "

Rather, God is calling husbands to lead in ways that please him. If, and I stress *if*, the husband tries to lead God's way, then God asks a wife to submit and try to let him lead. This doesn't mean that God thinks the husband is a better leader. It does mean that someone has to lead. Being a true leader is not an easy thing. It requires character, good judgment, selflessness, and integrity. In other words, followers are earned—not given.

It may appear that I have contradicted myself and am now arguing for male dominance. Before we have a mutiny and you throw me overboard, listen to the voice of experience. I have counseled hundreds of marriages in trouble. Many times I have heard stories of abuse and infidelity. Couples fight over money, sex, housework, and kids. But with few exceptions, 99 percent of all marriage troubles I have seen boil down to the same complaint. No, it is not an overbearing husband being the boss of the house. Rather, this is what I hear: The husband does nothing, and the wife has to do everything. What really troubles a home is when the husband wants to be the boss, but not a leader. I have heard countless tales from wives that their husbands control them, demand things, and throw tantrums. I have never heard a wife complain that her husband was too good a leader. In most cases today the wife is working, cleaning, raising the kids, paying the bills, and taking out the trash, while the husband sits with his shoes off watching TV.

> **" Today's society is not suffering from overactive husbands, but from absent husbands. "**

Having a husband who is actually a leader is a far-off dream for most women. Today's society is not suffering from overactive husbands, but from absent husbands. There may be a man in the house, but he is not the head, the leader, or even a helper.

Blame Catchers

Women have been given a bad deal. They carry most of us along for most of our lives, but they aren't allowed to lead a church service. They have shown themselves to be strong, responsible human beings, but they are made in certain quarters to submit to the whims of men.

Most of what has been taught in my absurd religion concerning women is just old-fashioned prejudice. It doesn't all come from men. Many women also believe that the Bible teaches a secondary place for females. But you don't have to be a Bible scholar to see that the Bible passages about women deal with cultural issues, not spiritual issues. Our culture is different now and without compromising biblical truth we can make adjustments for our own circumstances. This doesn't offend God at all; it pleases him.

As a pastor I constantly have to work within an atmosphere of prejudice against women in churches. Although I do not agree with it, that doesn't make it go away. So I am careful how I place women in ministry. I try to be wise in a culture of prejudice just as Paul was wise in his day. I try to give men and women a chance to adjust, so they can see for themselves the wonderful addition women are to the ministry.

Maybe someday we won't have to be so careful. But for now we must continue to deal with the absurd prejudice.

Ruth's Story

I knew God was calling me into the ministry since I was a child. Growing up female in the 50's and 60's didn't give me any ministry role models. A wonderful woman who had been doing mission work in South America began to speak to me about the saving power of Jesus Christ and prayed with me as I gave my life over to Him. This strong woman of God had preached to men and women in another country but when she came back to her own church she was only allowed to work with children. Of course for my sake, I'm glad she was ministering to children, but where is the justice in saying it's okay to preach and teach in another country, but not in America? Even though women filled most of the pews in the church, it seemed they were only worthy to teach children, play the piano or sing.

As an adult who loved God and wanted to serve him to the fullest, again, frustration became a part of my life. My husband was a pastor but even though I worked and sought God for the same purpose, I was never acknowledged as a pastor. Of course, we know it's not the title that's important, but again I could feel the restraints of prejudice coming against me as I would try to minister. So many in the church were controlled by their own deeply rooted prejudices.

Paul wrote in Galatians 3:28, "There is neither Jew nor Greek, slave nor free, male nor female, for you are all one in Christ Jesus." God's call is not based on race, social status or gender. If Christians are going to touch the world, there must be a lifting of the veil that has covered the eyes of the church in order to re-evaluate the role of women in ministry.

A friend told me to leave this chapter out.
"Jews won't listen to non-Jews," he said.
"You are wasting space," he told me. "Who wants
to read about the Jews? Nobody cares about
them." Maybe he is right, but I'm going to put
it in anyway.

CHAPTER TEN

ABSURD PREJUDICE—JEWS

A famous religious leader once said, "If I had to baptize a Jew, I would take him to the river Elbe, hang a stone around his neck and push him over with the words 'I baptize thee in the name of Abraham.'" He also said, "I shall give you my sincere advice: First set fire to their synagogues or schools and bury and cover with dirt whatever will not burn, so that no man will ever again see a stone or cinder of them."

Is this the ranting of some sick, anti-Semitic wacko? Some neo-Nazi cult leader? Or rather, are these the words of someone who is still revered and followed in my absurd religion? The latter, unfortunately, is true. These are the words of Martin Luther, the leader of the Protestant Reformation. These statements and others like them make it clear—Martin Luther had a real problem with Jews. And as the founding father of the Protestant Reformation, many of his ideas still influence the doctrines of many churches.

Luther's unfortunate influence has caused my religion to make Jews a separate class of people. It's almost as if everybody else in the world gets a shot at God's love, grace, and mercy, but my religion gives the Jews a cursed and bloody future. My absurd religion says the Jews rejected Jesus. Consequently, they deserve judgment—apparently for all time forward.

For five hundred years, from the days of Martin Luther until now, Protestants have been fixated on the idea that Jews are supposed to suffer. Compare the way Christians treat Jews with the way Christians treat other people. It is absurd prejudice.

" These Christians are willing to reach out to Buddhists, Hindus, and Muslims, but not to Jews. "

There are people in my own neighborhood who despise Jesus. Yet I see Christians taking cookies to them and inviting them to church. These Christians are willing to reach out to Buddhists, Hindus, and Muslims, but not to Jews. I also see ministries spending millions of dollars to send missionaries to foreign countries like India, Russia, and China. But I don't think I have ever heard of a "missions trip" to Israel. Christians go to Israel all the time, but they go as tourists—not as evangelists.

Jacob's Trouble?
Unfortunately, my religion interprets the Bible through its anti-Jewish prejudice. This is why most Christians had a "hands off" policy during the Holocaust of World War II. Many believed the Holocaust was supposed to happen and that the Nazis were sent by God to punish the Jewish people. Then, when Israel was grant-

ed statehood in 1948, many Christians called it a counterfeit Israel. This made it still okay to persecute Jews.

Today there is a lot of interest in when the end of the world will come, an idea we will talk about in another chapter. But what do the end of the world preachers say about Israel? They teach a doctrine called "Jacob's Trouble." It says that a time of terrible suffering will happen in Israel before Jesus returns.

These preachers believe that during Jacob's Trouble, two out of three Jews living in Israel will be destroyed. With the current population of Israel, that would mean 4,500,000 Jewish men, women and children. As the persecution of Jews increases, many Christians interpret it as a sign of the end and the return of Jesus. In other words, anti-Semitism is now a positive sign of the end times. Since many believe it is the will of God for Jews to suffer, the church has no motivation to stop it.

On the other side are Christians who are not anti-Jewish, but call themselves friends of the Jews, or friends of Israel. One pro-Jewish group helps Jews migrate to Israel. They raise money to fly Jews to Israel to live there. I think that is a great idea, but some of these Christians also believe in Jacob's Trouble. How could they put a Jewish person on a plane believing that two-thirds of all Jews living in Israel will be killed? Isn't that sending them to their deaths? If they believe in Jacob's Trouble, then they ought to be putting them on a plane and flying them the other way!

These ideas about the Jews flow from bad Bible teaching. Most end-of-the-world preachers take what Jesus said and put it two thousand years in the future. They act as if Jesus was talking over the heads of the people who actually heard his words, and was speaking instead to us two millennia later. Common sense alone tells us this is absurd. When Jesus said, "This generation will see these things," he meant the generation he was talking to at that moment. Can you imagine those people hearing his words and saying, "No worries. We'll be long dead before any of that bad stuff takes place"? Of course not.

> **" Are we foolish enough to believe that Jesus would talk about something that would happen two thousand years in the future, and not even mention the impending massacre? "**

Jesus warned them to prepare for a catastrophic event that would take place in their lifetime. It happened in 70 AD when the Romans destroyed Jerusalem. Some have estimated the death toll at more than 1,000,000. Are we foolish enough to believe that Jesus would talk about something that would happen two thousand years in the future, and not even mention the impending massacre?

Yet Christians today are still waiting for Jesus to return to Israel and judge them. The way I read it, Jesus returned to judge them in 70 AD with the destruction of the temple. So now, we can confidently say it is done. If my religion thinks Jews should pay for rejecting Jesus, then in my book they have already paid and shouldn't have to pay again. Protestants need to stop placing

Jews in "Double Jeopardy." Our society must stop seeing Jews as living in perpetual judgment.

In my absurd religion, most people actually believe that Jesus was against the Jews. Even worse, most believe that he was out to start another religion called Christianity. But Jesus wasn't anti-Jewish. He was anti-tradition. The religion of his day had allowed tradition to take over. Jesus was actually bringing Jews back to true Judaism. Later, non-Jews would join Jews in worship and claim Jesus as their Messiah.

I believe this is the pattern for our day. I want to see Jews and non-Jews together just as they were in New Testament days. But if this is ever going to happen, we have a lot of prejudice, ignorance, and absurdities to get past. My religion should be a positive influence on Jews and I have some ideas to get us to that point.

Holy Jealousy

First, Christians need to stop converting Jews. What I mean is Jews don't ever have to stop being Jews—even if they believe in Jesus as their Messiah. My religion needs to remember the sign placed over Jesus' head while he was on the cross. It said, "Jesus, King of the Jews." Jesus is the Jewish Messiah. Therefore, Jews remain Jews. They may become a different kind of Jew, but they will always be Jewish. There was never any question about this among first century Christians.

What should happen with non-Jews? Exactly what the Jewish Christians in Jerusalem taught in the first century: Non-Jews don't need to become Jewish. Jews remain Jews, and non-Jews remain non-Jews. Yet, we all come together under the one Messiah, Jesus of Nazareth.

Given these new ground rules, how can we Christians help Jews today? Not by screaming that they are all going to hell. That didn't help me before I became a Christian, and it won't help them either.

" Every Jew knows that the glory of God was at one time exclusively theirs. "

Rather, the New Testament says Christians are to make the Jews jealous. That's how we are supposed to help them. But what do we as Christians have that they might become jealous of? Let's take inventory. Is it our money that will make Jews jealous? No, they have just as much money as we do. Is it our backbiting, gossiping, in-fighting churches that will make them jealous? Ha! Will our cathedrals, schools, moral system, or theology make them jealous? I doubt that any one of them will.

I can only think of one thing that could make a Jew jealous. There's only one thing that has ever caused Jews to fall facedown before their God. What is that one thing? It is the glory of God.

Every Jew knows that the glory of God was at one time exclusively theirs. The Hebrew people were the only ones on the face of the earth who had it. It made the other nations tremble before them. It brought them success, prosperity and military victories.

On one of our several trips to Israel, Kathy and I decided to fly EL AL, the Israeli airline. Like everyone who flies that airline, you learn what it means to be subjected to Israeli security. The entire procedure took over an hour and a half. One of the reasons it took so long is that Kathy and I didn't travel to Israel with a group. We drove around by ourselves and visited friends. Understandably, they wanted to know where we would be going and what we would be doing.

They separated us from the other passengers and from each other and asked us many questions. Then we stood and watched the security people compare notes. Finally, back together, a young woman who appeared to be around 27 or 28 years old approached Kathy and me. She looked us over glancing occasionally at our passports. "Now, tell me again why you are going to Israel," she asked.

Kathy was getting impatient, so she got real with the young lady. She looked her straight in the eye and said, "Let me tell you a story. My husband, Steve, is the pastor of a church in Missouri. He worked and tried very hard, but it was a prejudiced small town, and the people were difficult to work with. Finally he could take it no more, and he left town. While gone, he searched his soul, and he searched for God."

"Two weeks later, he returned and parked in the same parking space that had been his for twelve years. There was no warning or sign that anything was about to happen. But when my husband walked into the area of the church where the congregation was worshiping, suddenly, like lightning from heaven, the hand of God touched him. It was as though heaven opened and

God's presence came down. I saw my husband become a different man—right before my very eyes. Everyone in the room was amazingly affected."

"Soon newspaper reporters came, and TV news crews brought their cameras. *Newsweek* magazine came, too. Over the course of three years, thousands and thousands of people came to our little town because they heard the glory of God could be found there."

" If God can touch a preacher in a tiny town, he can certainly touch a tiny nation like Israel. "

By this time tears were streaming down the face of that young Jewish woman. She looked at me and said the most profound thing: "Shouldn't that be happening in the Holy Land?" "Yes," I said, "and that is why we are going to Israel." With that she smiled and said, "Then come on through."

Her question, "Shouldn't that be happening in the Holy Land?" has changed my life. If God can touch a preacher in a tiny town, he can certainly touch a tiny nation like Israel. This is the answer for Israel spiritually, militarily and economically. It will do no good to offer them morality, theology, or worthless ideas like Jacob's Trouble. But, I can encourage the church to seek the glory of God and share it with its original owners. Then we will see the rescue of Israel, not its destruction. God can still show us his glory. He did it for me. He will do it for you. He is ready to do it for Christians and Jews everywhere.

Deborah's Story

As a Jewish person, I have always had a sense of despair, a kind of shroud of death. Anti-Semitism is so prevalent in religious teachings today, with no scripture base whatsoever. So it's a great challenge to put into words how I feel every time I hear anyone speaking with unmistakable love, concern, and confidence in God for not only Israel, but for Jewish people around the globe. That message conveys a great hope for all of us as it strips away every bit of gloom and doom.

Most Jews do not know that they just need to return to their covenant with God. They need to hear that God will come down and rescue them in times of trouble. He restores expectation and a future to the very people who, at one time, were the only ones in existence who had the glory and the presence of God.

Hearing such life-giving words of expectation has removed every sense of a fatalistic lot in life. I now live in a world of high anticipation of rescue for Israel and all descendants of the motherland who are scattered throughout the nations.

All Israel should hear this message of hope and a future.

As the threat of terror escalates, maybe others will believe and add their voices to mine. Hearts that believe, matched with the greatest military power in the world, would be unstoppable.

CHAPTER 11

ABSURD TERROR

I
t might seem odd to have a chapter about terror in a book about religion. Am I trying to convince you that terror or terrorists are absurd? I think that would be a waste of time and paper. However, if you look at how my religion faces the war on terror, it will become absurd. Let me explain how the two subjects relate.

The war on terror is not about land or money. It is not about one country wanting to invade another for a vast fortune. This war is rooted in spiritual concepts and not material things. It is a war about religious beliefs and principles. That's why it will never just go away. There is no land to lose or win. There is no line drawn in the sand. To the terrorists this war is about their god granting them their rightful place in this world.

Terror is not an act. It is an attitude. Terrorism cuts deep into the soul. It captures the conscience and distorts the mind. It crosses the line of reason into a place where negotiations do not exist. They can't exist. What is there to negotiate? How can a person negotiate what they believe? It is passed along patiently from generation to generation.

Americans, meanwhile, are almost buffoonish in their approach to terror and Christians are even worse. They misunderstand the entire conflict. My absurd religion thinks the entire world is serving the same God but using different names for him. Terrorists don't believe that. To them our God is false. We are pagan infidels.

"I believe that the American church is failing America in the war on terror by preaching a powerless God."

From where I sit, this is when religion gets absurd. Terrorists believe that their god will fight for them and they will win. But my religion makes its God a pacifist, like the young men who fled to Canada during the Vietnam War so they wouldn't have to fight. We have no concept of God fighting for us on the battlefield, or confusing our enemies or helping us to stand up for justice and peace.

One episode of The Simpsons says it all. With a comet racing towards earth to destroy the city of Springfield, Homer says, "It's times like this I wish I were a religious man." The Reverend Lovejoy runs by and says, "It's all over people! We don't have a prayer!" That's exactly where the American church is now. When our "holy" men and women are pushing a theology of disbelief in God's intervention, what hope is there of divine help? They have invented a God who uses psychology as his main weapon against people who have no desire to talk things over.

It amazes me that my absurd religion has such a strong voice of outrage against same-sex marriages but becomes like the "see no evil, hear no evil, speak no evil" monkeys when it comes to terror. It can lobby and legislate, rant and rave to protect our nation from being destroyed by the gay community, but when another religion threatens to kill innocent people, it gets laryngitis.

The God Advantage

Something is missing. The other side has a weapon we don't. The other side has an arsenal of faith. They don't just believe in a god. They believe in an active god who will make sure they win.

I believe that the American church is failing America in the war on terror by preaching a powerless God. The military does its part. Government, politicians, and Homeland Security all do their part. What is my absurd religion doing? It should be, like the prophets of old, teaching us how to activate the power of God. Instead, we are ignoring a major battle of our time and heading down to the courthouse to make sure we get to have our nativity scene again this year.

As a result, we are spinning our wheels in this war. Everybody is trying to move forward but we aren't getting anywhere. We have to live with our fingers crossed. We have the military and political strategies, but no spiritual strategy. Everyone is doing his or her part except those in the church.

How has religion failed America? By failing to provide the "God Advantage." If God's people follow God's plan they get the God Advantage. What is the God Advantage? Let me explain by telling a story.

Once upon a time, the king of Aram went to war against Israel. He set up his armies and waited for the Israelites to come near to catch them by surprise. The Israelites never came. He would try this place and that place, but the Israelites seemed to know his every move. Finally, enraged, the king decided there must be a traitor among his own advisors.

"Which one of you is a traitor?" he asked.

"None of us," said one of the officers.

The king didn't understand. Someone was indeed telling the Israelites his secret plans, but it was no traitor. It was Elisha, the prophet of Israel. The Aramean officers told the king as much.

"It is Elisha the prophet," they said. "He tells the king of Israel the very words you speak in your bedroom."

" Unfortunately, my absurd religion has failed to provide Americans with the faith to believe in a God who would actually do something to help us. "

You see, Israel had the God Advantage. They knew the plans of the enemy ahead of time. God went to war for his people. Historically, God has always done that. He gives the God Advantage to those who seek him with all their hearts. Unfortunately, my absurd religion has failed to provide Americans with the faith to believe in a God who would actually do something to help us. It has failed to present even the remote possibility that the United States could gain the God Advantage in this war on terror.

When the other side blows something up, they claim their god helped them do it, and they praise him. On our side when something does go right, there is no mention of God. He is not considered a player, not even by the church. Instead, we argue on the nightly news which political party or military strategy was responsible for a victory or defeat on the battlefield.

Our men and women on the battlefield should be given the God Advantage. Most of them have been around religion their entire lives, but all they know is a powerless God who leaves most people alone. Yet they are in the same war as our Bible heroes, fighting the same ancient evil.

When it comes to same-sex marriages and preserving what has been called our Judeo-Christian values, Christians are quick to stand up for what they believe. But don't expect a miracle from them. Don't expect the God Advantage. They wouldn't know where to begin. I feel sorry for our troops. I am sad that my absurd religion has prepared them so poorly for battle. Most will go into battle believing we all serve the same God with different names. How can they pray? To them it would be like asking God to choose sides.

Ancient Holy War

The most famous terrorist in the Bible is Goliath. He taunted and terrorized the Israelites every day for nearly six weeks straight. There was no one to stop him until David came along. Who was

David? He wasn't a military man. He was a shepherd. Yet he believed something that no one else in all of Israel believed.

He believed that God wanted to stop the terror. Most people think that David killed Goliath with a stone and a sling shot. David said he had something else. David said, "I come to you in the name of the Lord." Goliath laughed at David — but not for long.

" We have become a nation of cupcake preachers. "

Goliath was just one man, and today we face multitudes of Goliath's with bombs, rockets and guns. Soon we may even face terrorists with nuclear capabilities. We have the greatest military power in the world. Yet David had something then we don't have today. He had the name of the Lord. God killed Goliath through him. David was more than just willing to fight. He was God-empowered to fight. He had the God Advantage that my absurd religion is presently incapable of giving.

Everyone knows we are in a religious war. Terrorists call it a holy war. So where are our holy men? Where are our clerics and spiritual leaders who should be guiding us through this war? They are down at the coffee shop chilling out with a latte and telling folks that God loves them. Is that what God is saying to us as a nation, "Smile, I love you"? We have become a nation of cupcake preachers. Our religious men and women are more confused than King Saul was. He didn't know what to do about

Goliath and my absurd religion has no idea what to do about terror.

The fighting and hunting down of the world's leading terrorists has been difficult, frustrating and costly. The average American, although believing in God, has never even considered divine intervention as an option. Even sadder is the fact that it hasn't crossed most preachers' minds either.

Another way that my absurd religion has made terror absurd is in the area of negotiations. My absurd religion thinks God is a pacifist who would never pick a fight much less stand up for himself. It has no faith for even a modest God intervention. So with what does that leave us? It leaves us with negotiations. We want to sit down at the peace table and work something out. That's like a native American Indian chief smoking the peace pipe with the cavalry and expecting a fair deal.

" My absurd religion thinks God is a pacifist who would never pick a fight much less stand up for himself. "

You cannot negotiate with terrorists because they do not want to make peace. They don't want to strike a deal that is fair to everyone. They have no intention of sharing. They intend to destroy until what they are mad about is gone.

No wonder we have no peace in the Middle East. True terrorists don't want peace. If there is peace, there will be no reason to destroy. Haven't you ever noticed that when peace is

almost reached, someone on the other side blows something up
to end it? Terrorists want to destroy and annihilate. They want
whatever and whomever they hate to be gone.

God of the Battlefield

Back in 1899 Mark Twain wrote, "There's more than one way to
skin a cat." It means, of course, there are more ways than one to
get things done. I believe it is the responsibility of the religious
community of America to remind the world of God's many "cat
skinning" abilities.

Goliath wasn't the only terrorist in the Bible. He is just the
most famous. The Midianites were an entire nation of terrorists.
They terrorized Israel for seven years. God let it happen, too.
It would have been easy for Israel to think God was a pacifist
or maybe anti-war. No. Terror was happening to Israel because
their leaders had become corrupt in their religion. The religious
had tired of their own religion. God used the terror of the Midianites to get the attention of his own people. He got their attention and promised deliverance.

God chose a man by the name of Gideon to be a voice to
the people. Gideon was a nobody from a family of nobodies. He
questioned what God was asking him to do. Then he changed
course, believed and acted to unite the country and inspire his
countrymen to believe, too.

Gideon's first campaign was to fix his own broken down,
dead, idol-filled religion and replace it with God's kind of religion. God always requires us to do that first. God never goes out
to fight until his own people get interested in him again. Next,

the Spirit of the Lord came upon Gideon. I think we could use a little of that today, too, though first we'd have to peel the lattes from the hands of our holy men.

Now watch how God starts to skin the cat. Before there is even a battle, God starts sending bad dreams to the enemy. They interpret their own dreams and know that Gideon's God is coming after them. The enemy's army was as thick as locusts with more camels than could be counted. Gideon goes after them with just three hundred men. He gives each one of his brave fighting men a trumpet and an empty jar with a torch.

Three hundred men blow three hundred trumpets, smash three hundred jars and wave three hundred torches. Then they all shout as loud as they can. Some of the enemies run, crying out as they go. The rest of the enemy gets so frightened and confused that they pull out their swords and start killing each other. Not one soldier in Gideon's army died that day. I told you God has more than one way to skin a cat.

This story reveals just how inventive God can be. Gideon had more than a willing army and a military strategy. He had what we don't have. He had what my absurd religion has failed to give us. He had the power and presence of God working for him.

Maybe now you know why I called this chapter absurd terror. The terrorists aren't absurd. My religion is absurd and it gets even more absurd when it comes to terror. Don't be surprised to see most of its leaders running with the Reverend Lovejoy shouting, "We don't have a prayer." These are the people preaching from the pulpits of America that God doesn't do miracles anymore. Unless we get some champions back in our pulpits who challenge us to believe, Lovejoy just might be right.

Preaching Fear Out, Teaching Faith In

Fear is powerful. It is so powerful that without it terrorism doesn't work. Someone can blow something up, but it isn't terrorism if no one is afraid.

Fear comes naturally to most of us. Faith does not. God has always been in the business of turning our fears into faith. That's probably why in the Bible God always seems to be telling someone, "Fear not."

" God has always been in the business of turning our fears into faith. "

Think of what your life would be like without fear. Obviously, some fear is healthy— like the fear of a fast moving train. That kind of fear just might keep you alive. But most fears don't keep us alive. Most of our fears become debilitating to us in some way. Fear is a thief. It steals the life right out of you.

Almost everything I have ever feared has never happened. Most people's lives are locked up by the fear of things that will probably never happen.

What would your life be like without that kind of fear? What kind of person would you be? I suspect that most of us would have a different personality. We might even have different jobs or maybe we would have married different people. Fear is powerful. It is powerful enough to influence life's critical decisions.

What if all you had was faith? What if instead of walking by fear, you started walking by faith? My guess is that a faith-filled person would be unstoppable. A person who isn't afraid can't be terrorized.

" Without fear, there can be no terror. "

What is a terrorist? What is one made of? All terrorists are cowards pretending to be brave. They are cowards who strike innocent people. They are children throwing tantrums when they don't get their own way. They are manipulators who depend on fear to force what they want into being.

I believe it is the responsibility of ministers to instill faith into the souls of the American people. God told Joshua as he faced insurmountable odds to be strong and very courageous. God practically commanded Joshua not to be afraid. When Joshua did what God told him to do, "The walls came a tumblin'down."

The church should be preaching fear out and teaching faith in. Without fear, terrorists cannot exist—at least not as terrorists. Yes, they can still blow something up in a childish tantrum. However, they will never be able to take us captive or hold us ransom to our fears again. Without fear, there can be no terror.

Small-town Terrorists

Let me tell you how I learned about terrorism. I didn't take a course or travel overseas. This might sound strange, but I learned the basics of terrorism being the pastor of a small church in a small town. It sounds too far-fetched, doesn't it? Let me try to explain what I saw and what I experienced.

" We may be waging a war that we cannot win without God's help, even with our present weaponry and strategies. "

Certain people wanted to control the town and my church. They wanted to be the ones who decided what was acceptable and what was not. In fact, when I arrived to pastor the church, the building had a padlock on the door. Four years earlier the church was shut up tight and the pastor "pressured" to leave town. Some people didn't want it back open. When I opened it up anyway, that's when the small town terror started. No, they didn't blow up the building. Nothing so dramatic. Instead, they used fear, manipulation, threats, gossip and rumors to control. I know that gossip cannot be compared to blowing up a bus. But if you have ever been lied about or had everything you said twisted, then you know it's not funny. There were people who lived in and around that town who controlled it by ruining reputations. And these liars, gossips and controllers were all considered "good Christians."

It eventually started happening with a few of my own church members. I constantly faced people who wanted to control everything. When they didn't get their way, they followed the pattern of the town. They could lie, twist everything, and never feel bad about anything.

I would hear all kinds of things about myself. It was rumored that I was a cult leader, stole money from the church and was having an on-going affair for two years—all at the same time. No one ever asked me if any of it was true or false. No one cared. If I would call someone to ask why he or she was saying these things, they'd deny it all. They would tell me how much they liked me, hang up the phone and lie to someone else about what I had just said. How did I survive living there for twenty years? Here is what I learned:

- Don't be afraid. There is no power if there is no fear.

- Ignore them. Backstabbing cowards hate to be ignored.

- Build up your faith in God who has more than one way to skin a cat.

" There is no greater call than for my religion to rally our nation in faith for a secure future. "

Now, years later, I teach and talk about real terrorism—the blow-up kind. I help to free people from fear and teach people how to pray and talk to God in faith. I wish the news media would take my advice and not broadcast every threat these international terrorists make. Put their threats in an intelligence file and ignore them publicly. They don't deserve to have that kind of power to put fear in people's hearts.

All terrorism is a stench in the nostrils of God. It is cowardly control. I believe our nation should do everything in its power to hunt down those who kill innocent men, women and children. The use of Homeland Security, sophisticated intelligence and a strong military are necessary parts. However, without help from heaven, we may be in for a very long haul. Worse yet, we may be waging a war that we cannot win without God's help, even with our present weaponry and strategies.

As terror increases, so will the need of my religion to make the necessary changes so God will come down to help us. My absurd religion has gotten so far off the mark that it has become useless in this very real war we are fighting. It can promise nothing but a home in heaven if we die. In its present condition, it cannot offer us the power of survival in a world of terror.

However, if we would seek God with all our hearts, he would give us the God Advantage. There is no greater call than for my religion to rally our nation in faith for a secure future. We would experience his creative intervention in our battles, just like in the Bible. Then the world would see what happens when the God of justice, faith and goodness goes to war with us against our enemies.

Paul's Story

As a military person, I can say that there is a desperate need for our troops to hear about the God Advantage. I have been a military commander for 11 years, and I can tell you unequivocally there are no atheists in foxholes.

There is an altogether different attitude about God on the battlefield overseas than in a dead religious setting. The men and women serving overseas in the heat of the action are ripe for the truth concerning the living God. They know that something is missing. They need hope! They hear the enemy shamelessly shouting the name of their false god as they charge into battle. Our troops need to be given the REAL God—not a powerless, politically correct God.

Our troops desire a message that carries an authentic answer to the terrorism dilemma and genuine expectation that God will come down and rescue our troops.

A military backed up by God would send a shock wave around the world! Hope and integrity would grow and expand among our ranks with the presence of God. God's name needs to become our military's first weapon and line of defense—and the stage is set for it.

People believe different things when it comes to the end of the world. Some of my friends believe in the "rapture" of the church and some of them don't. Some believe the book of Revelation has already happened, but will still happen again. This is my attempt to take the "last days" out of the science fiction realm and into reality.

CHAPTER 12

ABSURD END TIMES GA GA

Maybe you've seen religious leaders on TV debating about the "end times." I sure have—and I always cringe. My absurd religion is obsessed with the end of the world. It's like the science fiction fantasy of the Religious Right. It makes a great fear-motivator to scare people into right behavior. It gets the attention of those who don't attend church. It also spices up otherwise boring sermons. Some preachers are one-note, end-times Johnnies. If it weren't for the doom looming on the horizon, they would have nothing to preach.

Unfortunately, my absurd religion doesn't always pay attention to what Jesus actually said about the end of the world. They love their end time ga ga. They love their "Left Behind" phobias. It's a multi-million dollar industry for authors, speakers, and filmmakers. It makes great entertainment.

Let me give you a brief history of the end times ga ga, so you can impress your friends at the next dinner party or potluck. The original Mr. Left Behind was a guy named John Darby. He lived in the early 1800's. He believed that Satan controls the world and that evil will completely take it over in the end.

Darby believed that God did do miracles in the past, but that his power is unavailable to us today. His ideas about the end times have been almost wholly adopted by the church today.

See if this sounds familiar: Darby believed Jesus will return to Earth not once, but twice. The first time he will snatch away all the Christians on the planet in a sudden and unexpected event dubbed "the Rapture," and the rest of the world will be left behind under the rule of the antichrist. Christians will stay with Jesus in heaven while evil takes over the world.

According to this theory, the world will then suffer beyond imagination. The antichrist will control the world and all of its resources. He will give a number to everyone. The number is 666. Anyone who does not receive the 666 mark will be killed. Then Jesus will come back a second time to judge the world.

Most of those who adhere to Darby's teachings are unaware of how new these teachings really are. They think all Christians have believed this way for two thousand years. The truth is that Darby's ideas are not found in any ancient writings and are only about two hundred years old.

Converted From Left Behind

It's confession time. I once convincingly taught the left behind theory. I taught it without giving it much thought. I taught what I had been taught. I viewed the end times through John Darby's theoretical lens. I read books by writers who were also reading through his lens.

Why did I believe the left behind idea without questioning? Why would I defend a two hundred year old idea so passionately? I, like countless others, had become a fatalist. I accepted the progression of evil as God's will. Therefore, I had to become an escapist, too. If you believe that evil is going to increase and eventually take over, then it helps to build a rescue mission from heaven into your theology.

" The idea of the antichrist coming and all the Christians leaving was such a nice clean end of the world package. I didn't want to mess with it. "

As a child, I attended the Nazarene and later the Methodist church. My family had never heard of a snatching away or a "rapture of the church." But when I became an adult, I started hanging out with Baptists and Pentecostals. They tried to scare the living daylights out of me! They saw signs of the end of the world everywhere. In the 70's there was an oil crisis. That meant Armageddon in the Middle East and the end of the world. During World War II, people thought Hitler was the antichrist, and in the 1980's I read it was the Pope. Now Christians are looking for a new candidate.

But one day I took a closer look at my end times theology. Actually, I developed a new interest in modern Israel and Jews, and what will happen to them. What I read in the Bible didn't seem to match what I was reading in most of the popular end of the world books being written. It wasn't an easy study for me.

I found Darby's ideas were deeply ingrained in my mind. The idea of the antichrist coming and all the Christians leaving was such a nice clean end of the world package. I didn't want to mess with it. But something didn't seem right, especially the part about the Jews.

Darby-following Christians taught me that God had abandoned Israel and the Jews, and they would be left behind to suffer with the rest of the sinners. But I read in the Bible that God doesn't forget Israel—ever. God said he would bring them back to their Promised Land. Didn't God do that in 1948, when in one day Israel was re-born as a nation? Did God do that only to make them suffer more? Why would I as a Christian get mercy, and they get none?

My friends all said it was because they had rejected Jesus and rebelled against God. But hadn't I done the same thing in my life? And God still had mercy on me. The Bible also says that when Moses led the Hebrews in the wilderness, water came gushing out from a rock, and that rock was Christ, or the Messiah. They rejected Jesus there, too. Yet, after one generation, God was faithful and brought them into the Promised Land. No doubt the religious Jews' rejection of Jesus as Messiah was a significant event. However, God has done it again. They are back in the Promised Land. Darby's idea of God rejecting the Jews for all these centuries was looking less likely to me.

Then I began to read books written by Bible scholars and people who know the languages and the history of the Bible. What did I discover? The greatest scholarly minds, at least those who are not writing to make money or please a denomination, are saying the same thing. They are saying that the book of Revelation is not a literal book. It is a book written almost in code to a generation that was to face the fierce Roman Empire. John wrote in code with wild descriptive language that only believers would understand. There was no way the Romans were going to figure out he was writing about them. It was a great way to tell believers that when it looks like the Roman beast is taking over, Jesus will win in the end.

I had heard this idea once before from someone, and my first reaction was to make the sign of the cross over them to protect myself. I liked my end-time ga ga. However, to take a book that so closely fits an event that has already taken place and transport its message two thousand years forward started to seem weak to me. I had no choice but to read on. Here is what I discovered:

In the year 70 AD, the most catastrophic event in Jewish history took place. The Romans destroyed the temple in Jerusalem along with an estimated 1.1 million Jews. The Jewish religion would never be the same. It was the end of Judaism as it had been known.

Jesus was warning his generation of the coming beast and destruction. They would see the end of an age, not the end of the world. With the exception of his actual physical return, his generation did see those events take place. It was not the end of the world, but it was the end of 2,000 years of Judaism as Jews had known it. Jesus himself said the temple would be destroyed. He told his followers what to look for and what to do when they saw these things.

Yet Left Behindists of today ask us to believe that the book of Revelation was written for us. They further ask us to believe that the Bible says nothing about one of the greatest catastrophes in Jewish history, the Roman destruction of the temple and massacre of the Jewish population. Talk about self-centered theology!

It became increasingly clear to me that the "end time" events recorded in the Bible were written to Jews of that day. We can apply the teachings, but they were not written for you, or for me, or anybody else living 2,000 years after that time period. The very idea is absurd. John, the author of the book of Revelation, wrote a message from God for the friends and family that he loved. He wrote to seven churches that are named and were in existence in his day. He warned of a beast who was coming. His number was 666, which can be translated as Nero, the Roman Emperor. It would be bad. It would be tribulation such as the Jews had never seen before. It would be a "Great Tribulation" that would last until Israel was born again as a nation in 1948. I hope all my "Rapture" theory friends can forgive me, but I'm pretty sure that's what the book of Revelation is about.

A Book For All Ages

But Revelation is also a timeless book. It's not just for then, and it's not just for now. Its purpose is not to warn us of a beast handing out numbers. It is a book that tells every generation how to think when up against a destroying beast. There have been many beasts in history, and that is why every generation believes the last book of the Bible applies to them. Evil will loom large again and again in this world. But we don't have to despair. We don't have to give way to fear or evil. God always remembers his people and is faithful to all generations. The message of Revelation is one of hope, not doom, from Jesus himself. God will win. Whatever generation you're in, don't give up. God will not let evil take over the world——even when it looks really bad.

" The idea that God actually stops evil rather than lets it take over is just the opposite of what most popular end-time preachers teach. "

The Bible, from beginning to end, shows the God who never gives up and never gives in to evil. Mankind failed in the garden, and there were consequences. But God never walked away.

Again, at the time of Noah, evil was everywhere. Yet God remained faithful to the world and rescued humanity through the ark.

Time and again God has saved our bacon. There's a strong pattern of this in the Bible. So instead of saying that the world will progressively become more evil and turn even further away from God, I think the Bible indicates that God will keep intervening to help us. Jesus said the Kingdom of God is among us. Surely this must mean the beginning of the end for evil. Of course evil will not end all at once, but little by little the Kingdom of God will grow like a mustard seed. The idea that God actually stops evil rather than lets it take over is just the opposite of what most popular end-time preachers teach.

Think of it in terms of the cross. Jesus didn't gain repossession of the world for free. He paid for it with his own life. And he is not giving it back—ever. God will never abandon what he created. He is not an irresponsible parent. He doesn't salvage what he can and abandon the rest. His creation is not evil. It is good and worth hanging on to. Though an evil outside force has invaded what belongs to him, God will remain in charge. Every generation will have its beast, but God will still be at his best.

What if there is no Armageddon in our future? What if it has already happened in the past and all end of the world stuff is science fiction ga ga? Many believe that the Armageddon of the Bible took place when Rome gathered in that valley before it destroyed Jerusalem. If that is true, then there is no need to run and hide. There is no need for escape. We might be on the very edge of global revival—not global collapse.

What about the end of our world? A careful reading of the Bible reveals that the world will not be destroyed by armies, or wars, or anything caused by mankind. God, like a good parent, remains in charge. The earth, God's good creation, will be transformed by God himself. At the end of the age, evil will be destroyed, not the world. The world will be made new.

The last days leading up to Earth's final transformation could see humanity at its finest—not its worst. Imagine that. Imagine ordinary people of all nations feeling as though heaven has come down to visit them.

How will we know the end is near? When will this age end, and what are the signs of its ending? Will the end come by nuclear explosion? World War III? A series of natural catastrophes? Shall we look for an evil satanic beast to rule the world until God finally destroys it all in judgment? No, the end does not come by disaster, trouble, or tribulation. The Bible says that the end comes by preaching.

Jesus said that when the gospel of the kingdom is preached to every nation, then the end will come. Notice he said "gospel of the kingdom," not the gospel of convenience that so many preachers advocate today. Jesus' statement tells us that when preachers shift from a self-centered gospel to the kingdom gospel, we will be closer than ever to the end of this age when evil will retreat once and for all.

The problem as I see it is that all of this end-time ga ga has become a distraction to the real message. What if it doesn't happen like some people think? In the meantime, millions are living scared of being left behind and afraid that the number 666 has been released like a virus on the Internet. Others live in a self-righteous escape mode mentality, unwilling to do anything to stop evil because they believe it is "supposed to happen."

I'd like to break the fascination with all ga ga and get on with reality. I was in it as deep as the next guy, so it has taken a lot to get me even to consider any other possibilities. At least for now, I am thinking in terms of blessing rather than destruction and it has given me a greater faith in the God who never gives up and never gives in to evil.

Greg's Story

I was raised in a Pentecostal church in the southern part of the United States. As a child, I was terribly fearful about the end of the world. It was practically impossible for me to escape the Cold War paranoia that was preached in American churches during that time. Some members of the little church I attended insisted the Bible taught that the Soviet Union was going to invade Israel around 1981.

Because of an erroneous interpretation of the book of Revelation, some assumed President Ronald W. Reagan was the antichrist because he recovered from a serious gunshot wound, and his first, middle and last names all had six letters, meaning "666." All this petrified me.

My Sunday school teacher was excellent at demonstrating the impending "rapture," when Christians go up, but sinners are left behind. She would carefully place two paper figures on a flannel board. Then, after quoting Matthew 24, "Two will be walking, one will be taken and one will be left behind," she would snatch one of the characters away.

"Will you be left behind?" she would ask. "I don't believe we have another ten years. Jesus is coming soon." It scared me into being good.

Sweaty evangelists in shiny, three-piece, polyester suits visited my church spitting out threatening words like bullets from a firing squad: "Sin can't fly! When the rapture comes, if there's sin in your life, you ain't gonna fly!"

These guest speakers would peer down the aisle to where I sat terrified. In an effort to escape their piercing eyes, I would try to hide behind one of the large columns nearby. I didn't want them to name my sin and cause me to be left behind during the "Great Tribulation." Spooky! But, there was one added thing that actually pushed me over the edge.

Sitting in the back seat of my dad's "In Case of Rapture This Car will be Unmanned!" vehicle, I read something that caused a cold chill to shoot down my spine. It was a book titled <u>88 Reasons Why the Rapture will be in 1988</u>, by Edgar C. Whisenant. This book made the future look hopeless. According to this man, I only had a few years to live. All I could expect was destruction.

I decide to embark on my own personal study of the Bible. I had to know what today's best scholars were saying we should expect. I was able to see beyond this catastrophic view of the world that religion had given me. Gratefully, I now understand that God is bringing restoration to his creation—not desolation. I am expecting a magnificent future!

So far, we've looked at a lot of the absurdities of religion. But, religion can be absurd-less. Now it's time for some answers.

CHAPTER 13

ABSURD-LESS ANSWERS

I was watching the evening news recently, when suddenly it was interrupted by the announcement that a person was missing and foul play was suspected. A massive manhunt was already underway and no expense or effort would be spared. His photograph was repeatedly splashed over all the television networks. How I wish I had a picture of God to put on the television screens of the world. God is missing from most churches, but I don't know too many looking for him. The Bible says to seek the Lord while he may be found. He can be found, but who is hunting for him?

The prophet Jeremiah in the Bible said, "No one asks, 'Where is the Lord?'" This is the question reporters and commentators ought to be asking our religious leaders—not where they stand on abortion, or whom they are supporting in the next election. "Where is the Lord?" My religion says he is here among us, but inactive and mute. I disagree. God has not changed. We have changed and God has chosen to move far away from us. Now we can't find him. My absurd religion either doesn't know he is missing or doesn't care.

Maybe when we get tired of living such dysfunctional lives, someone will ask, "Where is the Lord?" Perhaps when my religion gets weary of its own hypcrisy and moral weakness, it will ask, "Where is the Lord?" Maybe when the threat of nuclear terror is at our front door, someone will ask, "Where is the Lord?" When our troops are dying at the hands of people who claim another god, someone may finally ask, "Where is our God?"

I asked a small child in our church one time where God lived. He put his little hands on his heart and pointed as if to say, "In here." When kids talk about God, it is always cute. But my religion has grown men and women claiming that the God who created the universe lives inside of them. If that is true, shouldn't there be some sign or evidence of him being there? Even babies in the womb kick now and then. Is it too much to expect God to show us his presence—at least occasionally?

I was asked to be guest speaker once at a meeting advertised as a "contemporary youth service." When the music started, the young crowd began to chant, "God is in the house! Yeah, God is in the house! God is in the house, ya'll! God is in the house!" It was catchy, but I didn't see any sign of him being there.

Someone might argue that God is everywhere. Yes he is, but when God talks about his presence and when Jeremiah asks, "Where is the Lord?" it means an entirely different kind of presence. I am talking about his personal presence, when God shares his personal space with humans. He shows us his personality. His power is evidenced and experienced. The ordinary person walks away with a "God sense" that is real and life changing. That's the kind of presence I'm talking about.

Getting Used to Godlessness

I guess most in my religion have just gotten used to not having any evidence of God's presence. In Moses' day, the Holy of Holies was filled with the fiery presence of God. In Jesus' day, the Holy of Holies was empty, but the Jews carried on their religion anyway. One of the most remarkable gifts God gives humans is the ability to adapt. For example, in Missouri where I live, the summers can be blazing hot. When our friends from Canada visit in the summer, they look like they are going to fall over dead from heat stroke. After a while, though, they get used to it. They adapt.

But the ability to adapt can work negatively too. What do churches do when the presence of God can't be felt, heard or seen? They adapt. When God withdraws and becomes hard to find, what does it mean? It means he hopes someone will go looking for him. Instead, religion adapts like "empty nest" parents whose children have grown up and left home. It keeps itself busy with programs, promotions and politics, trying not to notice how quiet the house has become. Today many churches have sport groups, support groups, in-reach groups and out-reach groups—everything except God's presence. I think God is patiently waiting, hoping that somebody will finally notice his absence, stop compensating for the real problem and ask, "Where is the Lord?"

In the end, my religion has reduced Christianity to a group of powerless people trying to be moral. Their goal is to convert others to be moral along with them. Morals are good, but you don't have to be a religious person to have them. Christians are not supposed to be the people with a bunch of morals. They are supposed to be the people with a bunch of God. We are to be the people with His presence. Moses once asked what would distinguish God's people from the rest of the world if they didn't have his presence. Today's churches have lost their most valuable asset, God himself. He is displaced by political platforms and the psychologist's couch.

The Cost of His Presence

There is a cost to having God's presence. One day Jesus said to the crowds that if they did not hate their father and mother and family members, they could not be his disciples. That must have gone over like a lead balloon in a Jewish society that placed so much importance on family. Surely, Jesus didn't mean to hate someone, did he? Cupcake preachers today try to soften the blow and translate the word "hate" to mean "love less." They say it means to love Jesus more and everybody else a little less. But I don't buy that. Here is what I think it means:

Jesus was trying to make disciples. He was looking for disciplined, dedicated, committed followers. The would-be disciples were standing in the crowd, but who else was in that crowd? Their fathers and mothers, brothers and sisters, friends and relatives. Somehow, Jesus had to pull the future disciples out of that crowd to follow him.

I don't believe Jesus was calling men and women to hate their friends and relatives, but to hate what they stood for. They were going to have to hate the same old song and dance of religion that had become corrupt. The corruption was now affecting everyone spiritually, emotionally and economically. Jesus was trying to change the course of Israel's religion and the course of world history. The problem was that his future disciples were surrounded by loved ones encouraging them to keep going in the same direction.

My absurd religion is just like that. Denominations and leaders surround themselves with people who say all is well, keep going. We are not to hate people, but we are to hate what keeps society going in the same downward direction. This spiral cannot be stopped by human wisdom or invention. We must ask ourselves, "Where is the Lord? Where is his presence? Where is his glory and power? Where is the God of the Bible?"

What You Can Do

This book has tried to explain how my religion has become absurd and how it needs drastic fixing. My goal is to help normal people understand why the historic God of the Bible is nowhere to be found in most churches. What can be done? Can my absurd, broken, humanistic, anxiety driven religion be fixed? I think it can. Here are some points of recovery:

1. Having a good church is not the same as having a God church. Schools can be good. Sports can be good. TV can be good, but church must have God to be valid.

2. We need to define accurately the terms "salvation" and

"saved." Salvation means to be saved, preserved, healed and kept from harm in this life with the promise of eternal life. To be saved means that God's rescuing power is active in our everyday lives and affairs. How many people who claim to be Christians live that way?

3. My religion must start proclaiming the good news accurately and biblically. The good news is not about people going to heaven, though I believe in heaven and everything the Bible says about it. The good news is first about God coming to your house. The good news is embodied in what Jesus said to Zacchaeus the tax collector, "Zacchaeus ... I am going to your house today."

I daresay that most Americans have never heard the good news of the Bible. They have never heard that God will come down and heal our land. Yet that is the truly good news of the gospel. God still comes down to a hurting world. He still comes down to interact with humanity. He promises to become our healer, provider, protector and deliverer. In ancient days when God did not come down in times of crisis and need, it was up to the prophets to diagnose the problem, and call the people to respond to the remedy. If they listened to their prophets, God came down again. That's a roadmap for what we need to do today.

4. Religion must become God-centered. Christianity in America has become me-centered. It has learned how to turn self-centered preaching into cash. But the Bible makes it clear that a Christian is someone who is all about God.

I am no mental health expert, but as a pastor for thirty years I have sat and listened to people expose their inner lives. Here is what I have observed. The most mentally disturbed people I have met focus on themselves only. They talk as though they are the only person on the planet. Selfishness makes a person sick in every area of life. We are not meant to be me-centered.

5. It's time for an attitude adjustment. My religion doesn't get the same results that it did in the first century. I don't believe it is due to theological dispensations or because miracles ended with the Apostles. We don't get the same results because we do not have the same attitudes of first century believers.

Most leaders in my religion are frightened and disturbed by attitudes of excellence, sacrifice, commitment, generosity and devotion. Yet these are the things we need to get back and active. Why would he come down to a lazy, self-centered, mediocre, stingy, lackadaisical church? He won't, and he hasn't. We must adjust our attitudes to have success with God.

6. Jews and non-Jews must unite. Christianity can no longer be a separate religion from Judaism. What do I mean?

Jesus never stopped being King of the Jews. In the beginning, all Christians were Jews. Jesus, after all, was the Jewish Messiah. Through him, Jews were to be the light of the world. Followers of Jesus met in the same synagogues with other Jews and worshiped right along with them. Through signs, wonders and miracles, Jewish evangelists attracted

Jews and non-Jews alike. In fact, Jews did such a good job evangelizing that it wasn't long before non-Jews outnumbered the Jews. These converted non-Jews began to mix Greek and Roman ideas into their teaching. They interpreted the Bible through their experiences with pagan gods.

Then in 70 AD, with the destruction of Jerusalem by the Romans, many non-Jewish believers took that event as a sign that God was through with Judaism. The religion that Jesus worked for and died for was doomed to be replaced with a religious mix of Judaism, Christianity and Roman paganism. By the year 300 AD, Constantine made Christianity the official religion of Rome. From that time to our time, my religion has absurdly pushed away any Hebrew influence. To this day Christianity attempts to convert Jews away from the very religion that has been its foundation. Nowhere in the Bible does it say that Jews ever stop being Jewish. Christianity was supposed to be a revised Judaism and not a separate religion without any roots. It was meant to be Judaism reborn through faith in Jesus.

What can be done? God always works through people. A modern revival of the ancient presence of God will make my religion irresistible to Jews. We can stop trying to convert Jews to Christianity by telling them they will go to hell without Jesus. In fact, we won't even need to mention Jesus. Saul, a Jewish Pharisee experienced the power of God walking down a road. This caused him to ask, "Who are you Lord?" A voice from heaven spoke saying, "I am Jesus." If my religion can get the presence of God in our own lives, Jesus will speak for himself and do the rest.

7. Fire most ministers. We need new leaders with bigger goals than just cloning followers of dead religion or becoming the next mega big shot. Let's redefine what it means to be a leader in the church.

I was once asked to speak at a church that advertised itself as "refreshing, contemporary and different." The service started with colored lights that looked like they had been borrowed from a cheap bar. Next, smoke rolled in from the side of the stage. A guy came out with a guitar and sang "Amazing Grace" to the tune of the old sixties song, "House of the Rising Sun." There was nothing "refreshing" about this church. They took my same old absurd religion and tried to make it "groovy." That minister should be fired for insulting our spiritual intelligence.

Americans don't want "that old time religion." Neither do they want religious leaders trying to be cool. They want and need the presence of God. If a minister can't get the presence and power of God, then he needs to be fired. Replace him and his brethren with humble, teachable, bendable men and women who will do whatever it takes for America to have a fresh encounter with God.

8. My religion needs to change its tactics. It is waging a war it cannot win in its present condition. It fights for school prayer and against abortion and homosexuality. It stands up for family values. These are the wrong battles. Remember that the Jews fought against Rome in the late 60's AD be-

cause they thought God would help them win. They didn't know they had become estranged from God. They were living in a house built on sand.

My absurd religion is sick now like Israel was then. It is sitting on sand. Today's church is more concerned about who the next Supreme Court nominee will be than God's presence. It has misplaced priorities. When the storm comes, that house will fall with a big crash.

Our primary tactic should be to reconnect with the presence, power and provision of God.

9. We must have a real revival of religion that God will bless and be a part of. For the most part, the glory of the Lord has departed from religion in America. Since American evangelicals are the biggest "pushers" of religion, the deadness has spread around the world. The "Goliaths" of terror, poverty, famine and war can be stopped, but not without a big dose of God's power and presence. Is it too hard to imagine seas parting, walls falling, and men and women calling out to a God who hears and answers? I don't think so.

10. Hoop, Hip or Hype? Church, when done right, can be a wonderful time. People meet God face to face. Unfortunately, in my absurd religion, a God experience is a rare experience. The question is why?

First, the hoop. "Just say this prayer. Just be baptized our way. Just confess your sins." Beware of religion that promises eternal life by jumping through hoops. There is nothing simple about God. No one can "just" do this or that. Run away from those who cheapen Jesus.

Oh that horrid hip. Nothing is more sickening in my religion than a church that tries to reach society by being hip and trendy. Let's face it, the gospels were written two thousand years ago by people willing to die for what they believed. Dying for what you believe will never be hip. Flee the cool dudes.

Watch the hype. Beware of the exaggerated illustration. If it ain't happening in the people around you, it ain't happening. Some churches claim that signs, wonders, miracles, healings and deliverance happen as often as sunburn in the summer. These churches claim to have it all without any evidence. Exit immediately.

For me, I have no need for the hoop, the hype or the hip. I want to know what God is doing among the ordinary people. Look for a church that loves people enough to not let them be comfortable with who they are. Skip the church that offers warm and fuzzy religion. The real Jesus changes people quickly. Run to the church where the ordinary people believe, experience, know, and live in the very presence of God. You have found a real church.

CHAPTER 14

WHAT HAPPENED TO ME

The religion I turned to turned on me. My ministry, my marriage, and my family were in crisis mode. I wondered how we would survive the lies and rumors. How does anyone survive when church people turn hateful? I thought Christian love never turned on you. I thought I could trust these Christian folks with my life. My trust was about to get a rough education.

You see, in my religion, love doesn't mean forever. I know that now. In my religion, love is conditional. Some people apparently thought I didn't meet all of the conditions. I thought they loved me as their pastor. Instead, they became like the barking dog that wags its tail. I didn't know which end to believe. I just knew that one end was lying.

I thought that if I was as bad a person as these "good Christians" thought I was, shouldn't they be trying to help me? That wasn't going to happen. My religion is more comfortable playing the role of judge and jury. With them, trials are held at night, usually by telephone.

Somehow, we did survive and life seemed to go on for every-body—except me. My life was broken. My heart was broken. I just wanted out. I didn't want out as a Christian. I just wanted out of the lousy religious system that I had so naively trusted.

I don't want you to think that I was totally blameless. Not everything that had brought me to such a critical point was my fault, but some of it was. All I knew was I didn't want to be me anymore, and I didn't know what to do about it. I needed help, but my religion had so blinded me that I had no expectation that God would do anything in me. But then he did.

During this critical time in my life, the very hand of God touched me. That's right. In one moment, something happened, and I became another person. Not a perfect person. Just a different person. It happened right in front of about a hundred people or so. The presence and power of God became like lightning in my bones. I felt a surge of life coming out of me. It was as though the weight of my world and the baggage of my life suddenly lifted off me.

This experience changed my view of everything. For one thing, I became painfully aware that God hadn't been attending our church services nearly as much as I thought. Whatever it was that happened, I knew that my old religious life was gone, and there was no way I could ever go back. Something had ex-ploded on the inside of me.

But, how and why did it happen? What causes "God events" to happen to one person and not another? I was no saint, so I knew that being a saint wasn't a requirement. What made God reach out to me?

I think it was because I was so desperate to live and love again. I was willing to abandon all of my religious ideas and throw myself at God completely, no matter what. At the time, nothing else seemed to matter. I asked God to come to me, and he did. I know first hand what happens when God comes so very close. It is impossible for anyone to walk away unchanged. I began to understand God a lot better.

Who is Really Desperate?

The funny thing is this: Before my life crisis, I don't think I had ever really been desperate for God—even after years of ministry. I don't think I had ever been desperate for *anything* for that matter.

Sometimes, as a conference speaker, I will ask who in the audience is desperate for God. Hundreds usually respond. Are they desperate? I see them stand there with their heads bowed and arms folded saying they are desperate to find the living God. But it never works for them. They leave the same as they came. Let me share something that taught me what a real desperate person looks and sounds like.

I got an emergency phone call one day. There had been an accident. A little boy was hurt and the people on the telephone asked me to go to the hospital to pray with the boy's parents while he was in surgery. This was one of those friend-of-a-friend situations. I had never met the parents or any of the immediate family.

As I entered the ER waiting area, the room seemed in total chaos. People were packed together wall to wall. I couldn't tell who was whom. The hospital chaplain was already praying with a few people, and others were praying in small groups together. This was obviously a very religious family. I needed to find the parents, but didn't know what they looked like. Scanning the room, I tried to figure out who the little boy's mom and dad were. I walked a little farther—and then I heard it.

It was a sound like I had never heard before. Was it a cry or a moan or both? I wasn't sure what it was or where it was coming from. I turned the corner and saw a man praying with his fists. He and a woman were literally pounding the walls while making guttural sounds similar to words as they prayed. Right then I knew I had found the parents. I saw and heard real prayer that night, and I have never forgotten it.

Not long after that, I was praying the same kind of desperate prayers for myself. It was as though I was in a spiritual emergency room fighting for my life. I had my life-saving moment with God. I survived the crisis and went out to tell my story. I thought pastors, leaders, and religious folks everywhere would certainly want to know about this. I envisioned churches and denominations experiencing the power of God just as I had. I wanted to throw a spiritual birthday party for the entire world, jump out and yell, "Surprise! God still comes down to help his people."

To say I got a cold reception would be an understatement. I might as well have hired a stripper to pop out of a cake at a Moral Majority Convention. That's the kind of looks I got. Some believed, but some were suspicious. A few decided it was a publicity stunt. Fundamentalist evangelicals thought I was demon-possessed. The very idea of God actually doing something terrific terrified most preachers.

I was in a tough situation. Here was my dilemma: After twenty years of full-time ministry, something amazing, powerful, and life-changing happened to me. It changed the course of my life and the way I ministered. Soon, hundreds would come to hear me preach, hoping I might pray for them. TV shows had me as their guest; newspapers and magazines ran the story. Ordinary people came by the thousands from all over the world.

Isn't this what my religion has been praying to happen? Don't we want the world to come to our churches? You would think so. Instead, my religion showed its absurd hypocrisy and wanted nothing to do with me. That's when I saw it. That's when I knew it was true. My religion is drowning in emptiness with no intention of changing. It likes itself the way it is.

Rediscovering the God of the Bible

After that, it became increasingly more difficult for me to blindly accept what I saw in most churches. My religion has plenty of thrills and spills, fads and trends, but it is void of a powerful God. Commercialized Christianity has replaced God. Jesus is now our life coach and best friend. What I see mostly in my religion has nothing in common with the God of the Bible. To be honest, since that time when I experienced God's power, I have had a hard time finding a place where I can fit in.

In the Bible, a Jewish man named Saul, later to become Paul, was having a hard time getting his fellow Jews to accept an experience that was similar to mine. He decided that if the Jews refused to believe him, he would preach to the non-Jews.

This sounded like a good idea to me, too. Following his example, I decided that if church folks didn't want to listen, then I would turn to the non-church world and tell them what had happened to me. It was a good plan—except I had forgotten to factor in what religion in America has done to the minds and hearts of millions of Americans.

Instead of seeing what happened to me as hope for them, non-Christians became suspicious, thinking I must be another intolerant, judgmental gay basher or a get-rich-quick preacher. Their ears were so plugged up with disgust that it was difficult to get them to listen. However, when they did listen, when they realized that I am a religious insider who is just as disgusted as they are, everything changed. Their hearts opened and their eyes began to sparkle as they heard not about going down to hell, but about God coming down to them.

When I was back living and preaching in that small town, it was a challenge trying to grow a congregation. The building we had was old, built in 1859. The original stones piled one-on-one held up the floor. In the ceiling were beams put together by pegs instead of nails. We had no phone. The town had no gas station. The church had already been closed and locked up once, and I think most people thought it was only a matter of time before it would happen again. The idea that thousands of people would drive past endless rows of corn to get there seemed beyond impossible.

Yet, thousands did come. One newspaper estimated that 100,000 people had made their way to that church in 1996 and 1997. By 1999, it was estimated to be around 250,000. I will never know if those numbers are exact. I do know that on one particular weekend, 1,000 people showed up at one time. That means there were twice as many people showing up for church as there were in the entire town. We had to run a cable down the street for two blocks and open the Methodist church so people could watch on a big screen. We were experiencing things unheard of in modern times. Without announcement, van loads of visitors from Japan or Singapore or Australia would show up and stand in line for hours hoping to get inside. Explain that to me. Try to figure it out and nothing makes sense. What would make them come? What would make them keep coming for over three years to a small town of 532 people?

They came because God was there. They left there knowing that God wasn't in their churches as they had thought. I realized that people really do want God. What they don't want is religion with all of its absurdities.

As you know by now, I want to change all that. I think I can change some of it—if people will listen. If Christians would stop defending empty religion and non-Christians would stop being mad, together we might be able to change the world. I found out that the real God, the real thing, the God you read about in the Bible is near—really near. And you and I can have him.

I realize that I have said some things in this book that my religion doesn't want you to know. But they needed to be said. I think someone should have said them a long time ago. So let this be my contribution to humanity: to tell the truth about my religion. Now you know how it has treated me, controlled me, promised me everything and left me empty and alone. Then God came to me. I pray he comes to you, too.

Glossary of Terms Used

The Protestant Reformation was a 16th century reactionary movement within the Roman Catholic Church, largely provoked by Martin Luther, a Catholic Monk, when in October 31, 1517 he nailed his 95 Theses on the Wittenberg Church door in protest of certain church practices. Evolving from that time were various denominations and types of "protestant" churches. The word "reformation" has at its root the idea of "reforming" or "restructuring." The hope was a reformation or reworking of Church structure, practice and belief. Luther and his cohorts affected Christian Theology and belief systems that affect us still today and not necessarily in a positive way.

Repentance is usually defined as a "change of mind." While true it is only part of the definition. Christians tend to think being sad or sorry for sin is being repentant but this also fails to adequately define repentance. Biblical repentance is demonstrated in scripture when God's covenant people who have sinned are grieved and convinced enough that they confess their sin and turn back to God and ask to be not only forgiven, but restored to covenant again with Him. Being in covenant implies not only thinking differently but living differently as well.

Salvation is defined by most Christians as getting to go to Heaven when they die. The Bible teaches that to be "saved" has several inherent aspects among which are to be rescued, delivered, protected and helped. The biblical essence of salvation" means to help "now", as well as later, and that it involves the material well being of an individual as much as their spiritual life. Many Christians have been greatly influenced by Greek philosophy and its "dualism" which separates the "spiritual" and "physical" aspects of humanity to the point of making salvation all about a spiritual deliverance and a heavenly home. As saved Christians we are to be empowered by the presence of the Holy Spirit in us, enabling us to live overcoming lives in Christ on this earth, now, and to have the hope of bodily resurrection and a new body and new earth later.

The Gospel is another way of saying "the good news". The Greek word translated "good news" is *euaggelion*. In the New Testament you will usually find the "good news" they preached was about the Kingdom of God. *"Jesus went throughout Galilee, teaching in their synagogues, preaching the good news of the kingdom, and healing every disease and sickness among the people." (Matthew 4:23, NIV)* The true "good news" was that God had come down to earth as a man. Jesus Christ brought the in breaking rule of God's Kingdom into this fallen earth and conquered sin, sickness and death as a man. The result was that Jesus Christ makes His life and promises available to believers now.

Morality is, according to Webster, "conformity to rules of right conduct, moral or virtuous conduct." The question is of course who sets the standard for "right conduct." For those that believe in God and especially the Bible there is a biblical declaration of the will of God as to what is right or moral. Without a Judeo Christian basis or standard of right or wrong then people are left to set their own standards. These of course would change according to situation, culture or government and never be consistent. Only submitting to the will of God and His expressed Word gives us a firm, consistent and absolute standard of right and wrong.

End Times is a term referring to what is generally thought of as the end of or wrapping up of this present world order. The term expresses the belief that the world as we know it will come to an end. The idea of an end of things is widely held but how that end unfolds is largely contested and disputed. The apostle John wrote of a different order of things and the end of things as we know it. *"He will wipe every tear from their eyes. There will be no more death or mourning or crying or pain, for <u>the old order of things has passed away.</u>" He who was seated on the throne said, "<u>I am making everything new!</u>" (Revelation 21:4-5, NIV)* For the Christian there is not only an end to current ways but the promise of an ongoing and different future.

Steve Gray

Catapulted to national prominence in 1996 by a supernatural outpouring of God's power in Smithon, Missouri that ultimately drew over a quarter million people worldwide to his small-town church, Steve Gray has been visited by *TIME Magazine*, and featured by *Newsweek*, *Charisma*, The 700 Club, Trinity Broadcast Network and Daystar. A renowned author, his most notable works include *When the Kingdom Comes* and *Follow the Fire*.

Gray is also a pastor, conference speaker and musician, as well as the creator and executive producer of **The Steve and Kathy Show**. He is the founder and senior pastor of World Revival Church, and is also the founder of The House of Hope and Healing, World Revival School of Ministry and World Revival Network of Ministries and Churches in Kansas City, Missouri.

With over 20 years of full time ministry experience, Gray's unique insider perspective offers practical solutions that bring real change to America's churches, families and leaders. He is determined to meet the challenges facing the American church head on with his assertion that "Everyone deserves to experience the presence of God."

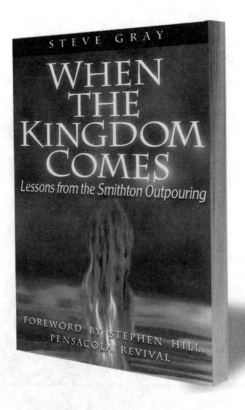